No Lex 10-12

PEACHTREE CITY
PLAN TO STAY™

Condoleezza
Rice

Other books in the People in the News series:

Beyoncé
Jamie Foxx
Angelina Jolie
Ashton Kutcher
Avril Lavigne
Tobey Maguire
Barack Obama
Queen Latifah
J.K. Rowling
Shakira
Tupac Shakur
Ben Stiller
Hilary Swank
Usher

Condoleezza Rice

by Anne Wallace Sharp

LUCENT BOOKS

An imprint of Thomson Gale, a part of The Thomson Corporation

THOMSON

™

GALE

Detroit • New York • San Francisco • New Haven, Conn. • Waterville, Maine • London

LIBRARY OF CONGRESS CATALOGING-IN-PUBLICATION DATA

Sharp, Anne Wallace.
    Condoleezza Rice / by Anne Wallace Sharp.
        p. cm. — (People in the news)
    Includes bibliographical references and index.
    ISBN 978-1-59018-521-6 (hardcover)
        1. Rice, Condoleezza, 1954—Juvenile literature. 2. Stateswomen—United States—Biography—Juvenile literature. 3. Women cabinet officers—United States—Biography—Juvenile literature. 4. Cabinet officers—United States—Biography—Juvenile literature. 5. African American women educators—Biography—Juvenile literature. 6. National Security Council (U.S.)—Biography—Juvenile literature. 7. African American women—Biography—Juvenile literature. 8. African Americans—Biography—Juvenile literature. I. Title.
    E840.8.R48S53 2008
    327.730092—dc22
    [B]

                                                                      2007024364

ISBN-10: 1-59018-521-8

Printed in the United States of America

Contents

Foreword   6

Introduction   8
From Birmingham to Washington

Chapter 1   10
A Child Prodigy

Chapter 2   23
Finding Her Passion

Chapter 3   33
Professor Rice Goes to Washington

Chapter 4   47
Provost Rice Advises the Candidate

Chapter 5   59
National Security Advisor

Chapter 6   73
Madam Secretary

Notes   87

Important Dates   93

For More Information   95

Index   98

Picture Credits   103

About the Author   104

Fame and celebrity are alluring. People are drawn to those who walk in fame's spotlight, whether they are known for great accomplishments or for notorious deeds. The lives of the famous pique public interest and attract attention, perhaps because their experiences seem in some ways so different from, yet in other ways so similar to, our own.

Newspapers, magazines, and television regularly capitalize on this fascination with celebrity by running profiles of famous people. For example, television programs such as *Entertainment Tonight* devote all their programming to stories about entertainment and entertainers. Magazines such as *People* fill their pages with stories of the private lives of famous people. Even newspapers, newsmagazines, and television news frequently delve into the lives of well-known personalities. Despite the number of articles and programs, few provide more than a superficial glimpse at their subjects.

Lucent's People in the News series offers young readers a deeper look into the lives of today's newsmakers, the influences that have shaped them, and the impact they have had in their fields of endeavor and on other people's lives. The subjects of the series hail from many disciplines and walks of life. They include authors, musicians, athletes, political leaders, entertainers, entrepreneurs, and others who have made a mark on modern life and who, in many cases, will continue to do so for years to come.

These biographies are more than factual chronicles. Each book emphasizes the contributions, accomplishments, or deeds that have brought fame or notoriety to the individual and shows how that person has influenced modern life. Authors portray their subjects in a realistic, unsentimental light. For example, Bill Gates —the cofounder and chief executive officer of the software giant Microsoft—has been instrumental in making personal computers the most vital tool of the modern age. Few dispute his business savvy, his perseverance, or his technical expertise, yet critics say he is ruthless in his dealings with competitors and driven more by his desire to maintain Microsoft's dominance in the computer industry than by an interest in furthering technology.

In these books, young readers will encounter inspiring stories about real people who achieved success despite enormous obstacles. Oprah Winfrey—the most powerful, most watched, and wealthiest woman on television today—spent the first six years of her life in the care of her grandparents while her unwed mother sought work and a better life elsewhere. Her adolescence was colored by promiscuity, pregnancy at age fourteen, rape, and sexual abuse.

Each author documents and supports his or her work with an array of primary and secondary source quotations taken from diaries, letters, speeches, and interviews. All quotes are footnoted to show readers exactly how and where biographers derive their information and provide guidance for further research. The quotations enliven the text by giving readers eyewitness views of the life and accomplishments of each person covered in the People in the News series.

In addition, each book in the series includes photographs, annotated bibliographies, timelines, and comprehensive indexes. For both the casual reader and the student researcher, the People in the News series offers insight into the lives of today's newsmakers—people who shape the way we live, work, and play in the modern age.

From Birmingham to Washington

In 1963, when Condoleezza Rice was nine years old, she and her family took a vacation to Washington, D. C., a city where African Americans were still discriminated against. Standing outside the White House, Condi turned to her father and said, "Daddy, I'm barred out of there now because of the color of my skin. But one day, I'll be in that house."[1]

Twenty-five years later, Rice was working long days as President George H.W. Bush's top advisor on the Soviet Union. And a mere ten years after that, she had a sunny corner office in the White House, a few doors away from President George W. Bush. By that time, Rice had become one of the most powerful female and African American figures in the world.

Her biographer, Antonia Felix, summarizes Rice's remarkable story:

> Condi has aimed for the top in every endeavor she has undertaken, and in most cases, she has succeeded. From a piano prodigy to a star scholar, esteemed professor to top Sovietologist, respected foreign policy official to award-winning author, university provost to president advisor, she is an icon of American achievement.[2]

Rice's success story takes her from the segregated southern city of Birmingham, Alabama, to the pinnacles of power in the nation's capital. Along the way, she forged a path for herself as a musical prodigy to the halls of academia and into an esteemed position as a Stanford University professor. Noticed by political insiders, she was then chosen to be President George H.W. Bush's top Soviet expert. After serving in Washington for two years, she returned to Stanford, where, as provost of the university, she erased the school's multimillion dollar debt and further enhanced her image. A strong friendship with the Bush family led her back into politics. After advising presidential candidate George W. Bush on foreign policy, she was chosen to be the first female National Security Advisor. After Bush's reelection, Rice became Secretary of State.

Despite these lofty positions, most historians and political analysts agree that Rice is not inherently ambitious. "Rather," as Nicholas Lemann observed in a *New Yorker* profile, "several of the critical turns in Rice's career have had the quality of an audition—she makes a big impression."[3] Historians Dick Morris and Eileen McGann elaborate on this concept: "The Rice style is clear: Tackle a subject, master it thoroughly and completely, perform at the highest level—preferably in front of movers and shakers—and then effortlessly become their protégé, accepting their mentoring on the path to power and success."[4] Rice's mentors have included several noted professors, a national security advisor, and two presidents of the United States.

With Rice as an important spokesperson for the George W. Bush administration, her every statement and action are in the public eye. She has been repeatedly praised for her efforts, but just as frequently criticized for her unwavering support of an increasingly unpopular president. She has received numerous death threats, while protesters have sought to prevent her from speaking on several occasions. Despite the criticisms and threats, Rice has persevered in speaking her mind and forging a position for herself in Washington and elsewhere. Felix summarizes: Whether it is in academia or politics, "Condi is a strong personality who is fully capable of holding her own...."[5]

Chapter 1

A Child Prodigy

Condoleezza Rice was born on November 14, 1954, in Birmingham, Alabama, a city that was, at the time, one of the most segregated in the South. A great-granddaughter of slaves, she was brought up believing that, although she was black, she could be anything she wanted to be. Despite prejudice and discrimination, Rice's childhood was a happy one, spent with two loving parents and in a supportive community.

She was named by her mother, Angelena, who had a profound love of music. The name "Condoleezza" comes from an Italian musical term, *con docezza*, which tells musicians to play "with sweetness." To her father, John, however, she was always his "Little Star," a nickname that he used well into her adult years. Most of her friends and other family members simply called her Condi.

A Remarkable Family

Part of the reason that Rice had such a happy childhood was that she had the good fortune to be raised by two dedicated parents who instilled in her a determination to succeed in a world that was largely prejudiced against her. Her mother, Angelena Ray, a college graduate, taught music and science at Fairfield Industrial High School in Fairfield, a predominantly black neighborhood of Birmingham. While there she met another teacher, John Wesley Rice, with whom she fell madly in love.

Condoleezza's father, John Rice, attended Stillman College, his father's alma mater, but he eventually transferred and graduated from another Presbyterian-based black college, Johnson C. Smith University in Charlotte, North Carolina. He received

A Remarkable Family Legacy

Rice comes from an extended family of college-educated African Americans that can be traced back several generations. Three of her great-grandparents were slaves, while her maternal great-grandfather was a white plantation owner who had several children with his black house slave. Julia Head, her paternal great-grandmother, was born into slavery and eventually married John Wesley Rice, a former slave from South Carolina who was able to read and write. They worked as tenant farmers in Eutaw, Alabama, and had nine children. One of the children, John Jr., left the farm and enrolled at Stillman College. Rice spoke of him in a speech given at the 2000 Republican Convention:

"George W. Bush would have liked Granddaddy Rice. He was the son of a farmer in rural Alabama, but he recognized the importance of education. Around 1918, he decided he was going to get book-learning. And so, he asked, in the language of the day, where a colored man could go to college. He was told about little Stillman College… So Granddaddy saved up his cotton for tuition and he went off to Tuscaloosa [Alabama]. After the first year, he ran out of cotton and he needed a way to pay for college. Praise be, as he often does, God gave him an answer. My grandfather asked how those other boys were staying in school, and he was told that they had what was called a scholarship. And they said, if you wanted to be a Presbyterian minister, then you can have one, too. Granddaddy Rice said, 'That's just what I had in mind.' And my family has been Presbyterian and college-educated ever since."[1]

After the Civil War, many freed slaves became sharecroppers or tenant farmers.

1 Quoted in "Condoleezza Rice Delivers Remarks at Republican National Convention." *Washington Transcript Services*, August 1, 2000.

both a bachelors degree and a masters degree in divinity from that college in 1951 and became the minister at Westminster Presbyterian Church in Birmingham, Alabama. John Rice also taught at the high school, coached basketball and football, served as a guidance counselor, and was very active in community affairs. He helped, for example, to set up the area's first Head Start, a program for minority preschoolers that prepared them for school. Historians Dick Morris and Eileen McGann summarize: "To say that John Rice was a tireless youth leader and educator is an understatement."[6]

John and Angelena both wanted a family and married in the early 1950s. Biographer Antonia Felix describes the marriage: "[Their] marriage brought together two family lineages that believed strongly in religion and achievement through education."[7] There were three generations of college-educated family members on both the Ray and Rice sides, a very rare occurrence in the segregated South.

Rice's extended family had always believed that education was the best way to succeed in a white world. In an interview later in her life, Rice reflected on her grandparents and other relatives and their legacy to future generations: "They had broken the code. They had figured out how to make an extraordinarily comfortable and fulfilling life despite the circumstances."[8]

A Musical Prodigy

Part of that fulfilling life was a love for music, something that had always been one of the dominant factors in Rice's mother's life. As a result, Angelena was determined to offer the same kind of opportunities to her daughter. Rice and her mother spent long hours exploring every aspect of the world of music together.

With both parents working during Rice's early years, she spent most of her weekdays with her grandmother Mattie Ray, a piano teacher. Condi spent endless hours watching Grandma Mattie and her students, and she comments on what happened as a result of these hours of listening: "So she [Mattie Ray] said to my mother, 'Let's teach her to play.' I was only about three—and as a result,

I learned to play very, very young."[9] Music became a central theme of her life—a theme that continues to the present.

Rice was a particularly good student and loved playing the piano from the first time her fingers touched the keys. The first song she learned to play was *What a Friend We Have in Jesus*. Before her feet could actually reach the piano pedals, Condi was playing Beethoven and Bach. In addition, she could also read music before she could read books. According to historians Morris and McGann, she gave "her first performance … at the age of four, at what she describes as a tea for the new teachers in the Birmingham public school system."[10]

When she was ten years old, her parents enrolled Condi in a local music school, the Birmingham Southern Conservatory of Music, a school that had only recently opened its door to African American students. The teachers there taught Condi new and

Condoleezza spent much of her early years with her grandmother, Mattie Ray (the woman in pink in the photo), who taught her to play the piano.

Music is an Important Part of Her Life

Rice's love of music developed early in her childhood and has not diminished over the years. Despite the fact that she now often works twelve- to fourteen-hour days, she somehow finds time to keep up with her musical practice and playing. In addition to playing quietly at home, she is a member of a chamber music group in Washington, D. C. Historians Morris and McGann elaborate: "She matured into a world-class concert pianist, a skill she retains to this day."[1] As a result of her skills, she has also been honored to play with several well-known and noteworthy musicians.

She was invited, for instance, in April 2002, to play a classical duet with world-renowned cellist Yo-Yo Ma. During a ceremony in which President Bush presented the cellist with the National Medal of Arts and National Humanities Medals, Rice performed and received a standing ovation at Constitution Hall in the nation's capital as the duo played Brahm's *Violin Sonata in D Minor*. She has also played with famed Malaysian violinist Mustafa Fuzer Nawi at a gala dinner on July 27, 2006. Additionally, Rice has appeared and played the piano on the CBS television show *60 Minutes*.

Rice performed a duet with renowned cellist Yo-Yo Ma.

1 Dick Morris and Eileen McGann. *Condi vs. Hillary: The Next Great Presidential Race.* New York: Regan Books, 2005, p. 66.

advanced piano skills, while also introducing her to the worlds of the flute and the violin. She was encouraged to enter piano competitions, an arena in which she excelled. Years later, Rice humbly reflected on her years of piano lessons. "I don't ever remember thinking I was an exceptional student. I did think I was a good pianist."[11]

"I Knew my Baby was a Genius"

In addition to being somewhat of a musical prodigy, Condi was also a particularly bright child. According to her Aunt Genoa McPhatter, "She was an early reader, and she always had a mind of her own."[12] As an only child, Condi received all of her parents' attention. Biographer Felix elaborates: "John and Angelena showered their daughter with love, attention, praise, and exposure to all the elements of Western culture—music, ballet, language, athletics, and the great books."[13] Condi loved not only what she was reading and studying but also developed a lifelong thirst for ever more knowledge.

Condi learned her alphabet and other skills while still a preschooler. She became an avid reader at a very early age. When she was five years old, her mother wanted her to start school, but a local principal refused to accept Condi, citing that she was too young to enter school. Angelena Rice refused to accept his opinion, taking a leave of absence to teach her daughter at home. In addition, her parents took her to Southern University in Baton Rouge, Louisiana, for psychological testing. The results proved Angelena had been right about her daughter's intelligence. Condi's mother later told friends: "I knew my baby was a genius."[14]

Condi did very well in school. In fact, she was so gifted academically that she was able to skip both the first and seventh grades. Because of her intelligence, she got bored easily, especially in situations where she felt her time was being wasted. She needed more advanced challenges to keep her interested.

Adding to her need for challenges was the fact that Condi was more mature than her years even in elementary school. Friends believe that this early maturity is attributable to her parents, who treated Condi that way at home. "They [John and Angelena] never talked to her like she was a child," states friend Moses Brewer, "which is why she was mature beyond her years."[15] This maturity showed itself in Rice's study habits and her determination to make the best grades in every class she took.

While she made friends easily and enjoyed playing with them, Condi far preferred to spend her time inside, reading and playing the piano. During her childhood she also took ballet lessons, learned to speak French, and became a very competitive ice skater. Whether it was academic or extracurricular activities, Rice gave 100 percent of herself to become the best possible student and athlete.

"Walk Proudly in Public"

Condi's achievements in her academic endeavors and other activities, however, were heavily influenced by the times in which she lived. The 1950s and 1960s were years when prejudice and

Birmingham, Alabama, was once considered one of the most segregated cities in the South.

discrimination against African Americans were at their peak. The civil rights movement was in full swing, with protest marches and sit-ins occurring across the South.

Growing up black in the South, Rice was always aware of these factors. Living in Birmingham, a city that many historians have called one of the most segregated in the South, racism was particularly apparent. The city, in fact, was dotted with "white only" signs. Blacks, for instance, were prohibited from going to the circus and to the local amusement park; nor could they attend white schools or eat in white-only restaurants. African Americans were also forbidden from voting in the South.

On one occasion, while shopping with her mother, Condi experienced this discrimination first-hand. She wanted to try on a dress but was told that she and her mother would have to go to a storage room to do so. The dressing rooms were for whites only. Angelena Rice refused this demeaning order, threatening to take her daughter elsewhere until the clerk reluctantly relented. Determined to give their daughter a "normal" childhood, her parents instilled pride and dignity in her, and as one biographer notes: "She was instructed to walk proudly in public and to use the facilities at home rather than subject herself to the indignity of the colored facilities in town."[16]

Despite these and other restrictions, Condi lived a full and rich life. Many people have incorrectly assumed that growing up in the segregated South somehow deprived her. Rice herself staunchly denies this assumption: "My parents had me absolutely convinced that—you may not be able to have a hamburger at Woolworth's, but you can be president of the United States."[17]

"It is a Sound I'll Never Forget"

In addition to facing daily discrimination, Condi, like other blacks in the South, also had to contend with violence. Violent acts against African Americans were common occurrences, especially in black communities like the one where the Rices lived.

The struggle for black equality became personal for Rice on September 15, 1963. She and her family were attending a

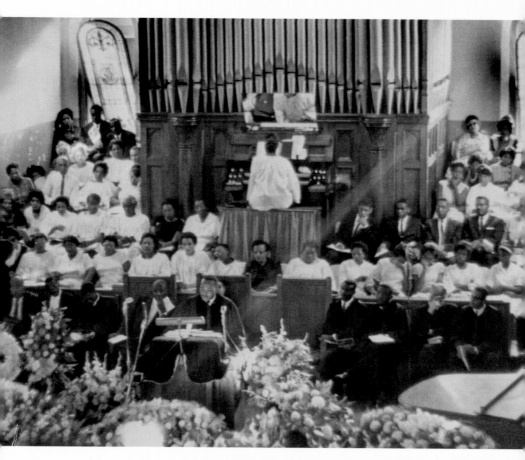

One of the four little girls killed in the Birmingham church bombing in 1963 was a friend of Condoleezza's, and the event left an indelible impression on her.

church service when the floor under her feet began shaking. The Sixteenth Baptist Church, a short distance away, had been bombed by members of the Ku Klux Klan, a violent anti-black organization.

Four little girls were killed in the bombing, including one of Condi's friends, Denise McNair. The children, ranging in age from eleven to fourteen, had been in their Sunday school classroom when the bomb exploded. Rice spoke of that day thirty years later: "I remember the bombing of that Sunday school... I did not see it happen, but I heard it happen, and I felt it happen, just a few blocks away… It is a sound that I will never forget, that will forever reverberate in my ears."[18]

Later, Rice and her family attended the funeral service for the girls. Rice vividly recalls that day: "I remember more than anything else the coffins, the small coffins. And the sense that Birmingham wasn't a very safe place."[19]

The events that day were forever burned into Rice's memory, and, in May 2004, she spoke of them in a commencement address to Vanderbilt University graduating seniors. She told the students,

> The crime was calculated, not random. It was meant to suck the hope out of young lives, bury their aspirations, and ensure that old fears would be propelled forward into the next generation. But those fears were not propelled forward, those terrorists failed.[20]

In addition to contending with church bombings, blacks in the South also faced violence in their schools and neighborhoods. Condi and her friends, for instance, missed countless days of school because of bomb threats in the mid-sixties. Most of these bombings occurred as a backlash to federal court orders to integrate the South's schools.

Many homes were also bombed, placing residents of black neighborhoods under the constant threat of violence. Groups of armed whites frequently drove through African American communities shooting and starting fires. When a bomb landed in their neighborhood, Rice's father reported it to the police. The police, however, failed to even conduct an investigation. To counter the violence and police inaction, John Rice and other fathers in their Titusville neighborhood patrolled the nighttime streets armed with shotguns and other weapons to keep the Ku Klux Klan out. Years later, Rice would admit that this experience made her a staunch opponent of gun control.

These experiences also propelled Rice to become even more determined to overcome adversity. In 2004, she talked about growing up during the civil rights era:

> I know what it means to hold dreams and aspirations when half your neighbors think you are incapable of, or uninterested

in, anything better. I know what it's like to live with segregation in an atmosphere of hostility, and contempt, and cold stares, and the ever-present threat of violence, a threat that sometimes erupted into the real thing.[21]

Rice credits her parents for helping her during these turbulent times.

I am so grateful to my parents for helping me through that period. They explained to me carefully what was going on, and they did so without any bitterness… Among all my friends, the kids I grew up with, there was … no doubt in our minds that we would grow up and go to colleges—integrated colleges—just like other Americans.[22]

St. Mary's Academy

The prejudice and violence that the Rices faced on a daily basis factored into their decision to leave the South. In 1968, when Condi was fourteen years old, she and her parents moved to Denver, Colorado, where her father took a position at the University of Denver. In addition to holding a number of administrative positions there, John Rice helped establish the university as a black intellectual center by teaching courses in African American history.

Her parents, determined to provide Condi with every possible educational advantage, enrolled her in a nearby Catholic all girls' school, St. Mary's Academy. She was one of only three black students at the school, her first experience with integrated schooling. She was surrounded by other students who shared her sense of competitiveness, whether it was in music or in academic studies. Rice thrived on the challenges.

In addition to excelling at school, Rice also continued her piano and music studies. While in Denver, her parents gave her an expensive, used Steinway grand piano for her birthday, a piano she still possesses and uses frequently. This gift allowed her to practice the piano at home. During her senior year in high school,

A Love for Sports

Rice's fascination with and love for sports came from her father, a former football coach. As a result of interaction with her father, Rice developed a lifelong love of football. She once stated: "My dad was a football coach when I was born and I was supposed to be his all-American linebacker. He wanted a boy in the worst way. So when he had a girl, he decided he had to teach me everything about football."[1] From the age of four on, she would cuddle with her father on the couch and watch football on television.

While in college, Rice became engaged to Denver Bronco football player, Rick Upchurch. At the National Football League games, she sat with the players' wives and enjoyed all the benefits of being an insider to the professional game. Despite the ultimate breakup of the relationship with Upchurch, Rice has remained a lifelong fan of professional football.

Rice has maintained her profound interest in sports. On February 2, 2007, she appeared on an ESPN television show and was interviewed about the upcoming Super Bowl. She came across as very knowledgeable about the game of football while competently analyzing the two competing teams. She has publicly stated that her greatest ambition in life is to become the NFL commissioner, a job she briefly considered in 2004, only to take the post of Secretary of State instead.

1 Quoted in Antonia Felix. *Condi*: *The Condoleezza Rice Story*. New York: New Market Press, 2002, p. 47.

Condi entered a young artist's piano competition and won. Her prize was to play a performance with the Denver Symphony Orchestra, a momentous thrill for the teenager.

Enjoying her academic and musical activities, Condi admitted that her high school years were relatively easy ones. By the time she entered her senior year, for instance, she already had enough course credits to graduate. Her parents wanted her to skip the year and go directly to college, but Condi insisted on finishing with her class. She recalls that time in her life: "It was the first time I ever really fought my parents on anything. I just had a sense that socially you're supposed to finish high school."[23] In addition to her high school coursework, she also took two college courses during her senior year from the University of Denver.

With her high school work nearly done, Condi, like all of St. Mary's seniors, met with a guidance counselor to talk about her future. Despite Condi's excellent grades, her counselor did not think she should go to college. Historian James Mann recounts the incident: "A guidance counselor tried to tell her she was not college material, but Rice ignored the advice."[24] Appalled at the counselor's prejudice, she was more determined than ever to succeed in life. She graduated from St. Mary's at the age of sixteen, near the top of her class, fully intending to continue her education and become a concert pianist.

Chapter 2

Finding Her Passion

Following graduation from St. Mary's Academy, Rice wanted to attend the Juilliard School of Music in New York City, a prestigious institution devoted to training the finest musicians in the world. Her parents, however, encouraged her to enroll at the University of Denver and live at home for at least a year or two. Her father, in particular, was concerned that Rice might change her mind about her career, stating that he wanted his daughter to have an all-around college education before transferring to the New York school.

Rice heeded her parents' advice and enrolled as a music major at the University of Denver's Lamont School of Music. Enrolled in all honors courses, the sixteen-year-old was convinced that she was headed for a career centered around the piano and her musical abilities. As part of her musical education, sophomore Rice attended the Aspen Music Festival. The event was a turning point in her young life. As she listened to eleven- and twelve-year-old prodigies, she realized that she was not good enough for the concert stage. She recalls: "I met eleven-year-olds who could play from sight what had taken me all year to learn."[25] She later acknowledged, in fact, that she didn't want to spend a lifetime teaching piano or being less than the best in her field.

As a result of this realization, when she started her junior year, Rice dropped her focus on music and signed up as an undeclared major. At this point, she had no idea what her future would hold, so she left her options open. She did know, however, that she wanted to be in a field where she could excel.

"It Was Like Love"

Her search for a new major led Rice to enroll in a wide variety of classes in her junior year, hoping something would catch her interest. She recalls that she was bored taking government classes and hated English literature. She was still uncertain when she decided to attend a lecture given by Professor Josef Korbel. The topic of the day was dictator Josef Stalin and the Soviet Union. She sat mesmerized as the professor talked of communism and Russia. That lecture changed her life. As she listened, Rice knew immediately that she wanted to study international politics and, in particular, hoped to learn more about the Soviet Union.

The turning point in Condoleezza's life came when she attended a lecture on Russia and communism given by Professor Josef Korbel (seated).

In making this decision to study the Soviet Union, Rice had found her passion. She remembers: "It just clicked. I remember thinking, Russia is a place I want to know more about. It was like love… I can't explain it—there was just an attraction."[26] The study of Russia and politics ignited a yearning in the young scholar that exceeded even her passion for music. She would later comment on this feeling when she spoke at a commencement ceremony at Boston College on May 22, 2006,

> I was lost and confused, but one day, a wonderful thing happened. I wandered into a course on international politics taught by a Czech refugee who specialized in Soviet stud-ies… With that one class, I was hooked. I discovered that my passion was Russia and all things Russian.[27]

When she told her parents that she was switching her major to international politics, her father was skeptical. Her aunt, Genoa McPhatter, explains: "Her daddy looked at her and said, 'Condoleezza! Black people don't make money in political science.' Rice replied: 'Music, neither.' "[28]

"A Dazzling Mentor"

In pursuing her newfound passion, Rice asked Josef Korbel, a Czechoslovakian by birth who had lived through both Nazism and communism, to be her advisor; he also became her mentor. Impressed by Rice's intelligence and enthusiasm, he took her under his wing and encouraged her to join the school's interna-tional relations program. She has, in the years since that time, repeatedly credited Korbel with leading her into a rewarding career in international politics. Rice explains: "I really adored him. I loved his course, and I loved him. He sort of picked me out as someone who might do well."[29] Journalist Guy Raz elabo-rates about Rice's relationship with Korbel: "To Rice, Korbel was a dazzling mentor, the person she cites as having inspired her to become a diplomat."[30]

Part of that inspiration came through attending Korbel's lectures where he taught his students about the way in which politics

Josef Korbel

Josef Korbel, a Jewish Czechoslovakian by birth, fled his native country after the 1939 Nazi occupation. Although he was on the list of Jews to be arrested, he was able to obtain visas for himself and his family to escape. More than twenty of his extended family members would later be killed during the Holocaust. He spent most of World War II in London as an advisor to Eduard Benes, the exiled Czech president. After the defeat of Germany, Korbel was a member of the Czech delegation to Paris for the peace conference in 1946. He then returned to his homeland and became the ambassador to Yugoslavia. After the Communist takeover in 1948, he and his family found refuge in the United States.

Korbel ended up in Denver in 1959 where he founded the Department of International Relations at the University of Denver. The author of six books, Korbel died in 1977, a few years before his student, Condoleezza Rice, completed work on her PhD. Korbel also served as a mentor to his daughter Madeleine Albright, who would become the first female Secretary of State, during the Clinton administration.

Madeleine Albright was the first female Secretary of State, under President Clinton, and was also the daughter of Professor Josef Korbel, Rice's mentor.

influenced different responses by governments. Having served as a Czech diplomat before, during, and after World War II, Korbel was a fascinating teacher, offering personal insights into the world of foreign policy and the effects of both Nazism and communism. Rice eagerly absorbed everything her teacher offered. She speaks of his classes: "He was a wonderful storyteller and very attentive to his students. It was that attentiveness, plus his ability to weave larger conceptual issues around very interesting stories, that made him such a powerful teacher."[31] After her parents, Korbel became the most influential person in her life.

During her study of international relations, Rice decided to focus her primary studies on the Soviet Union. She studied Russian music, culture, history, and politics. She also began learning the Russian language, a particularly difficult language to learn because of the complex Cyrillic alphabet. (The Cyrillic alphabet is an unusual-looking alphabet that uses symbols, signs, and letters, many of which are not found in the English alphabet.) Most students have to study Russian for years before even gaining a moderate understanding of it; Rice, however, grasped it almost immediately. Biographer Felix summarizes the importance of being able to read and speak Russian: "Month by month, Condi's increasing grasp of the language gave her a more intimate connection to the land that would become central to her life and work."[32] She was also a frequent visitor at Korbel's home, where the two of them had lively political discussions about world affairs.

Outstanding Senior Woman

As she studied the Soviet Union, Rice's junior and senior years at the University of Denver flew by. While her Russian studies occupied most of her time, she always found an hour or two each day to pursue her continued passion for music and the piano. She was also a member of the honor society, Phi Beta Kappa, wrote for the school newspaper, and, for exercise, spent her early mornings at the skating rink.

At graduation ceremonies for the nineteen-year-old, Rice was given an award for her outstanding accomplishments in the field of political science. She was also named the university's outstanding senior woman. University officials stated that this was "the highest honor granted to the female member of the senior class whose personal scholarship, responsibilities, achievements, and contributions to the university throughout her university career deserve recognition."[33]

Many years later, Rice addressed the graduating students at Vanderbilt University in Tennessee and spoke of her graduation. She stated,

> "It's been many years since my undergraduate commencement at the University of Denver. I remember almost everything about it—the pride of my family, the closeness I felt to my classmates and friends, the thrill that comes with reaching an important goal."[34]

The future looked bright for the young scholar.

An Obsession with All Things Russian

Following graduation, Rice decided to continue her study of international politics at the University of Notre Dame in Indiana, a school with a very prestigious Soviet studies department. During the early 1940s, Notre Dame had initiated one of the first government and international studies departments in the United States. After World War II and during the beginning of the cold war, the university became an important center for the study of the Soviet Union and the worldwide spread of communism.

While at Notre Dame, Rice came under the tutelage of another mentor, Professor George Brinkley, a Soviet expert. He recalled Rice as someone well versed in Russian history; he felt she was ready to enter an advanced study program. Brinkley stated, "Most students had little background [in Russia and Soviet studies], so we had to teach them basics... But she was extremely bright, so she came better prepared than most students."[35]

Because of her aptitude, university officials created a special program for Rice—an independent study that would challenge the young scholar more than regular seminars and classes. Professor Brinkley explains: "I could see that she was someone who was so highly motivated, and who had also read a tremendous amount, that she would benefit from a lot of opportunities to work on her own."[36] Rice would ultimately do far more independent study than any other student at the university. Working directly with Brinkley, the two would settle on a topic and then develop a reading list that was highly focused and individualized.

During her master's work, Rice studied the cold war and the ways in which the Soviet Union used its power. She focused specifically on the Soviet military and its intervention in Eastern Europe. Felix writes of Rice's continued devotion to her studies: "Condi's attraction to Russia, the Russian language, and the Soviet Union had blossomed into an obsession by the time she entered grad school."[37]

Rice graduated with her master's degree in government on August 8, 1975, at the age of 20. She moved back to Denver and lived with her parents, where she gave piano lessons, participated in the church choir, and enjoyed various sporting events with her father. She briefly considered going to law school, but Professor Korbel suggested she become a professor instead. She decided to take Korbel's advice and entered the University of Denver in 1976 for the purpose of obtaining her doctoral degree.

A Soviet Expert

After re-entering the university, Rice asked Professor Korbel to take her under his wing again. They enjoyed a very close working relationship until his death in 1977. Rice spent the next year taking various courses at the University of Denver. Biographer Felix explains what happened: "The courses she took that year made her realize how much she enjoyed analyzing the big issues and seeing how this analysis is put into practice to literally change the world."[38] Rice put all thoughts of law school aside and concentrated on obtaining her doctoral degree.

Her doctoral work focused on many different subjects—military history, Soviet foreign policy, international politics, and

A Dream Come True

Rice's trip to Russia was like a dream come true for the young scholar. It gave her an opportunity to experience, first hand, the culture and society that had ignited her passion. Speaking of that passion, she stated: "Culture is something you can adopt, and I have a great affinity for Russia… There is something about certain cultures that you just take to… It's like love—you can't explain why you fall in love."[1]

While in the Soviet Union, Rice was able to experience many aspects of Russian culture and history. She visited the Kremlin and saw the walls that added such an aura of secrecy to the government. Perhaps her best moment, however, was standing in the concert hall where one of her favorite musicians, Peter Ilyich Tchaikovsky, conducted his symphonies.

As an American black woman, Rice was well received in Russia. Treated with respect and some curiosity, she was able to talk to ordinary Russians in their own language and learn something of their lives. That Rice was treated well came as no surprise to St. Petersburg native Dmitri Gerasamenko, who stated: "A black student from a prestigious American university who could speak Russian would have been treated with much hospitality and respect."[2]

Peter Tchaikovsky is one of Rice's favorite composers.

1 Quoted in Antonia Felix. *Condi: The Condoleezza Rice Story.* New York: New Market Press, 2002, p. 86.

2 Quoted in Felix. *Condi: The Condoleezza Rice Story,* p. 109.

the history of communism. Rice's dissertation, a long, nearly book-length manuscript required of all doctoral students, was about comparative military regimes, specifically the relationship between the Soviet and Czechoslovakian armies, a subject she would later expand into a book. Her dissertation was entitled "The Politics of Client Command: The Case of Czechoslovakia 1948–1975."

To research her topic, Rice made a seven-week trip to the Soviet Union, where she gained a unique perspective on Russia and communism. This trip was a real treat for Rice. Always fascinated by her studies, she was now experiencing firsthand many of the things that she had only read about. Seeing the Kremlin and the places where some of her favorite musicians had performed brought Russia alive for her. In talking with people on the street and in government, she gained an insight into the Soviet Union that she could not have gained through the books she read.

In addition to her trip to the Soviet Union, Rice also did brief internships at both the Department of State and the Pentagon in Washington, D.C. These experiences gave her an inside look at the inner workings of government. Additionally, she did a brief internship with the Rand Corporation, a giant foreign-policy research organization. She had the benefit of working with some of the most knowledgeable experts in the field of foreign policy and Soviet relations. Rice received her doctorate on August 14, 1981, at the age of twenty-seven.

The Development of Rice's Political Beliefs

During the course of her academic studies, Rice was heavily influenced by Hans Morgenthau and his concept of *realpolitik* or power politics. Morgenthau was an international relations theorist and the author of *Politics Among Nations*, credited by most historians with being the American "bible" of post–World War II thinking about United States diplomacy. Like Morgenthau, Rice believed that nations act in their best interest and will fight, even go to war, to protect such interests. Rice supported the view that a country's most significant resource was the military, but she also saw the need for morality in decision making. Where others saw the cold war as a struggle between democracy and communism, Rice believed it was based on the conflicting interests of two competing superpowers—the Soviet Union and the United States.

During the years that Rice spent studying the Soviet Union, many exciting and crucial issues were being hammered out as the United States dealt with the communist threat. These events only added to her appreciation of what she was learning. The cold war, for instance, was in full swing, the space race was on, and several major treaties were signed, limiting nuclear weapons. With her understanding of the Russian language, Rice was able to read about many of these events in the Soviet newspaper, *Pravda*. In fact, according to biographer Felix, "One of the reasons Condi became a Soviet expert was the fact that it was a hands-on, ever-changing field in which history was being rewritten every day."[39]

Rice's studies and developing beliefs also influenced her voting record. In 1976, the year she enrolled in her doctoral program, Rice voted for the first time. She registered as a Democrat and then voted for Jimmy Carter. She quickly became dismayed, however, with his foreign policy after the Soviet invasion of Afghanistan. Although Carter restricted the sale of grain and technology to the Soviet Union, Rice believed that the president had not responded strongly enough. Rice comments:

> I thought it was time to have a tougher policy toward their repressive [Soviet citizens had few civil rights and freedoms] regime… I might never have changed parties were it not for what I thought was our mishandling of the cold war… I thought Carter didn't understand the true nature of the Soviet Union, which was pretty dark.[40]

During the 1980 presidential election, she switched to the Republican Party and has been a staunch Republican ever since.

Chapter 3

Professor Rice Goes to Washington

Following the completion of her doctoral work, Rice accepted a research fellowship at the Center for International Security and Arms Control, commonly known as the Hoover Institution, at Stanford University in Palo Alto, California. As an expert on Soviet affairs, Rice joined other scholars, businessmen, politicians, and foreign policy experts in exploring various international security issues. This fellowship came with a $30,000 stipend that was to last for one year.

Rice made such an impression at the Hoover Institution, however, that the university decided to utilize her skills in an additional way. Journalist Arthur Herstein describes what happened next: "Just a few months into the program ... she was singled out by the faculty and offered a teaching position... The position would last three years and could be renewed based on her merits."[41] She started as an assistant professor but soon became a committed teacher and, in 1987, was promoted to associate professor.

Professor Rice

Rice, one of the few African American professors at Stanford, quickly became one of the university's most popular and respected teachers. Her classes were always well attended and the students spoke glowingly of her teaching. One graduate student spoke of why Rice was so popular: "Her command for guiding our discussions and ensuring our eventual arrival at major

Rice was a popular teacher at Stanford.

conceptual understandings was outstanding among the teachers I had at Stanford."[42]

Most of Rice's classes dealt with military issues, international foreign policy, and national security. Biographer Felix elaborates on her teaching methods:

> One of her favorite teaching methods was to have her students re-create major foreign policy decisions in a series of role-playing sessions. Each student played a particular figure... She felt that role-playing helped students grasp the importance of the key players' personalities.[43]

As a professor of political science at Stanford, Rice would win two of the school's highest teaching honors. In 1984, she received the Walter J. Gores Award for Excellence in Teaching, and in 1993, the School of Humanities and Sciences Dean's Award for Distinguished

Teaching. In the award presentation, Provost Albert Hastorf praised Rice for her enthusiasm and love of teaching, as well as the curiosity for knowledge that she imparted to her students.

"Her Potential Seemed Boundless"

Despite her love of teaching, in 1986, Rice took a brief leave of absence from Stanford in order to go to Washington, D.C. Once there, she worked with the Joint Chiefs of Staff, the highest military advisory board in the government, on issues related to nuclear strategic planning. She was well received in the nation's capital. Historian Mann elaborates: "To powerful people, those at the top of America's foreign policy leadership, Rice was refreshingly different, and her potential seemed boundless."[44] She served as Special Assistant to the Director of the Joint Chiefs of Staff, under whom she studied nuclear planning. She immersed herself in the military culture found at the Pentagon and thrived. She later told reporters that her year at the Pentagon was one of the greatest experiences of her life.

Despite its difficulty, Rice quickly learned Cyrillic, the Russian alphabet. Here, the top line is written in Cyrillic.

Hoover Institution and Rand Corporation

The Hoover Institution of Stanford was founded in 1919 by Herbert Hoover, who would later become president of the United States. A former Stanford graduate, Hoover saw the need for a research center that could study international politics. Beginning as a place where documents on the causes and consequences of World War I were stored, the Institute gradually grew in size and scope until it held one of the largest archives and libraries in the world. The Institute, formally known as the Hoover Institution on War, Revolution, and Peace, is devoted to studying politics, economics, political economy, and domestic policy.

The Rand Corporation is also a research organization. Formed in 1948, this nonprofit institution, according to their website is "dedicated to furthering and promoting scientific, educational, and charitable purposes for the public welfare and security of the United States."[1]

Rice served internships and was on the Board of Directors of both organizations. She has repeatedly praised her years spent at these "think-tanks" as instrumental in helping her formulate her own views of foreign policy.

1 About Rand. "History and Mission." *Rand Corporation.* www.rand.org/about/history

Herbert Hoover, who later became President of the United States, founded the Hoover Institute of Stanford University as a place to research and study international politics.

While in Washington, Rice also served on the Council of Foreign Affairs, a group that publishes the journal, *Foreign Policy*. The goal of the Council is to increase the public's awareness and understanding of the world and international politics. The Council is also responsible for making policy suggestions to the government. Rice's knowledge of the Soviet Union was invaluable to her work with this group. Rice worked for both organizations during the Reagan administration at a time when the president was instituting a massive military buildup.

"Somebody I Really Want to Get to Know"

Upon her return to Stanford, Rice resumed her normal schedule of classes. As a professor, Rice also attended many meetings with influential people and policy makers. In the late 1980s, General Brent Scowcroft, former National Security Advisor to President Gerald Ford, attended a dinner meeting and roundtable discussion on the issue of arms control. Rice was in attendance and her comments deeply impressed Scowcroft. As various government heavy-weights discussed the pros and cons of arms control, Rice freely challenged their views and spoke her mind. Scowcroft later commented, "She was thoughtful, she was good, she wasn't intimidated, and I thought, this is somebody I really want to get to know."[45] Scowcroft, after listening to Rice, realized that the young professor had a profound knowledge of Soviet ideology and policy. He said: "She saw where we could cooperate and where not."[46]

Following the dinner meeting, Scowcroft decided to learn more about Rice by attending one of her classes. Her lecture on missiles and other long-range weapons helped convince him that Rice would be a powerful ally and asset for the national security team he was in the process of forming for presidential candidate George H.W. Bush. When Bush was elected president in 1988, Scowcroft, who was appointed National Security Advisor, immediately contacted Rice. He asked her if she would be willing to take a leave of absence from Stanford and work as a Soviet expert on the National Security Council, under his leadership. She accepted immediately, notified the university of her intentions, and moved to Washington, D.C.

Years later, Scowcroft talked of his decision to appoint Rice as an advisor on Soviet affairs:

> I had chosen Condi because she had extensive knowledge of Soviet history and politics, great objective balance in evaluating what was going on, and a penetrating mind with an affinity for strategy and conceptualization. She ... was up-to-date with military affairs.[47]

"An Inside Player"

Because the late 1980s were a critical time in the relationship between the Soviet Union and the United States, President Bush needed Soviet experts in his administration. The two countries had long been embroiled in a cold war, as each tried to exert its influence on countries around the world. Rice's expertise on and knowledge of the Soviet Union quickly made her an important person in the Bush administration. Mann elaborates: "From the very start of the first Bush administration, at the age of 34, Condoleezza Rice was an inside player."[48]

In 1989, Rice took her position as Director of Soviet and Eastern European Affairs on the National Security Council. She was uniquely qualified for the position because of her extensive background in Soviet and communist history and her ability to speak Russian. One of her earliest jobs, for instance, was to prepare a report on Soviet leader Mikhail Gorbachev, someone whom she had already been studying for years. Gorbachev was the Secretary-General of the Soviet Communist Party and, as such, was responsible for all domestic and foreign policy. Rice's thoroughly researched report, and especially her emphasis on the fact that Gorbachev was a reformer and someone the United States could work with, was then used by the president as the basis for American policy with the Soviet Union.

Rice also advised the president that the Soviet Union was in the midst of a domestic and political crisis brought on primarily by a severe economic depression. The Soviet government, Rice reported, was on the brink of collapse. She encouraged the president to use Russia's tenuous position to American advantage. Scowcroft reports:

> Condi reminded us that the Soviet Union was in the midst of domestic turmoil and was looking to the outside world for ideas and resources to rebuild its failing system. It appeared we might be able to take advantage of that situation to make dramatic progress across the entire United States–Soviet agenda.[49]

Rice further advised the president to cement American relationships with its allies in Europe, while also encouraging him to offer support to the East European countries who were beginning to challenge communist rule.

Interaction with the Russians

As President Bush's leading advisor on Soviet affairs, Rice was intimately involved in all decisions that related to the Soviet Union. She helped prepare the president for four summit meetings with Gorbachev, while also organizing a seminar of Russian scholars and experts who helped her in briefing Bush. At the first summit meeting with Gorbachev, in introducing Rice, the president told the Soviet leader, "She tells me everything I know about the Soviet Union." Acknowledging Rice, Gorbachev answered, "I hope you know a lot."[50]

Rice, in fact, did know a lot about what was happening in the Soviet Union. In her work as the president's primary Soviet advisor, Rice made sure that Bush was fully aware of the events that were occurring in Eastern Europe and elsewhere at the time. Dissatisfaction with communist rule in East Europe was rapidly rising. Leaders of the Soviet Union in the past had always responded to such problems with military force, but Gorbachev decided not to send in troops. Instead, he initiated two new policies: *perestroika*, or restructuring, and *glasnost*, or opening. As part of these policies, Gorbachev began to decrease the number of

Soviet troops in Eastern Europe. Partly on Rice's advice, President Bush decided to take a "wait and see" attitude.

Both Rice and Bush watched carefully as Poland became the first Eastern European nation to challenge Soviet rule and authority. In early 1989, the nation broke away from communist domination under the newly emerging Solidarity party. Rice advised the president to send economic and other forms of aid and assistance to the former communist nation to assist them in their stand against the Soviet Union. Bush and Rice, soon thereafter, traveled to Poland, where the president made a speech that had been written by Rice. In the speech, the president promised support and financial assistance to any emerging democratic movements within the communist European bloc.

The End of the Cold War

A few months after Rice and the president returned to Washington, they watched as the Berlin Wall, erected in August 1961 between East and West Berlin, fell on November 11, 1989. The East

Rice's first trip to the Soviet Union gave her insight into the people and the country she could not have gained otherwise.

Germans were allowed, for the first time, to cross freely over into democratic West Berlin. This event heralded a remarkable and shocking series of events.

Soviet leader Gorbachev asked for a meeting with President Bush to discuss the ramifications of what had happened in Berlin. Meeting in Malta, the two leaders' most urgent task was

Brent Scowcroft

Rice credits Scowcroft with bringing her into government work and facilitating her success in the first Bush administration. She worked closely with Scowcroft during one of the most tumultuous times in American history—the end of the cold war. Rice has praised Scowcroft for his mentoring and friendship.

Brent Scowcroft, National Security Advisor for both President Gerald Ford and President George H. W. Bush, was responsible for bringing Rice into the first Bush administration.

Scowcroft is best known for having served as National Security Advisor under both President Gerald Ford and President George H.W. Bush. A lieutenant general in the Air Force, he also served as military assistant to President Richard M. Nixon. He held numerous military positions and taught at both West Point and the Air Force Academy. Scowcroft received the Presidential Medal of Freedom in 1991, along with an honorary knighthood from Queen Elizabeth II. During his later political career, Scowcroft was a leading Republican critic of the American policy toward Iraq.

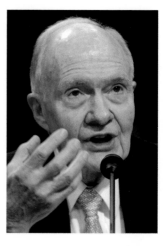

The fall of the Berlin Wall was the symbol of the end of the Cold War. Rice worked hard to help with the reunification of Germany.

to make decisions about the future and possible reunification of Germany. Rice was among those who advised Bush to push for a peaceful and gradual transition. She sat with Bush and Gorbachev at the large conference table where the two leaders nailed down an agreement allowing for the two countries to reunite.

After Malta, however, rather than moving slowly, the events leading toward reunification took place with amazing speed, leading to the first free elections in East Germany in March 1990. In the months following the fall of the Berlin Wall, Rice made many trips to Germany to help with the reunification of that country. She stated years later, "German unification was perhaps the most important issue of this entire period ... because that is where the cold war began, and that was the only place that the cold war could end."[51]

Rice watched with interest as between the end of 1989 and 1991, the crisis in the Soviet Union continued to escalate. She advised the president to tread very carefully, lest any American action undermine Gorbachev and what was happening in Russia. Historians Morris and McGann expound on Rice's role during this turbulent time: "Rice's focus throughout the first Bush administration was on balancing the superpower relationship, reuniting Germany, reducing armaments, and managing the transition out of the cold war."[52]

Rice later admitted that no one in the American government could have predicted what happened next. The Soviet Union quite simply fell apart. A power struggle developed at the highest levels in the communist government over the direction the Soviet Union was taking. Hard-line communists were alarmed at the reunification of Germany and the loss of their Eastern European satellites. In addition, many of Gorbachev's opponents were also upset that he had given the Soviet people more freedom and had begun a series of reforms. Other opponents believed his efforts were not enough.

Gorbachev's primary rival was Boris Yeltsin. As the crisis intensified, Yeltsin's power increased and he began to openly challenge the Soviet leader and his policies. Staunch communists were also tired of Gorbachev and launched a *coup d'etat*, an

Off-campus Activities

During her time at Stanford, Rice slowly built a life outside her work on campus. She played the organ at a nearby church, followed football as passionately as she always had, and worked out with Stanford physical fitness trainers. Biographer Antonia Felix elaborates on her off-campus life: "She juggled classes, advising, research, writing, playing the piano, weight training, exercising, dating, and gluing herself to the TV for 12-hour football watching marathons."[1]

Twice a week, Rice also played with a chamber music group, composed of Stanford musicians, who from time to time gave concerts on campus. Paul Brest, a Stanford colleague and violinist, spoke of Rice's participation in this group: "She's a real team player. You have to do that if you're playing chamber music."[2] She also attended piano and music workshops during the summers.

Rice dated occasionally, a Stanford University coach among them. Rice had a fairly long relationship with San Francisco 49er football player Gene Washington, with whom she has remained good friends. Other than a brief engagement to Denver Bronco player Rick Upchurch, Rice has never been engaged or married.

Rice has been a great football fan since she was a little girl.

1 Antonia Felix. *Condi: The Condoleezza Rice Story*. New York: New Market Press, 2002, p. 127.

2 Quoted in Felix. *Condi: The Condoleezza Rice Story*, p. 181.

attempt to overthrow the government. The coup failed, but the turmoil allowed Yeltsin to oust Gorbachev and eventually replace him as president. Meanwhile, many of the Soviet republics took advantage of the chaos and broke off from Russia.

Like Rice, many Americans watched with amazement as their old adversary, communist Russia, disintegrated. Rice, with her extensive background of Soviet history, also viewed the events that were occurring with great interest. She acknowledged that she felt privileged to have participated in the making of history.

"I Wanted a Life"

In March 1991, not long after the fall of the Soviet Union, an event that heralded the end of the cold war, Rice decided to leave Washington and return to teaching. Many of the former Eastern European communist countries had moved toward democracy, Germany had been reunited, and the Russians had even voted for the first time in their history. Rice spoke of those amazing years: "Events were unfolding so quickly that you would make a policy or make a decision or arrange a meeting and before you could get there, everything had changed."[53]

Citing that she didn't want to reach burnout in what she called an "all-consuming job," Rice decided to return to Stanford. She had been working fourteen-hour days, leaving little time for anything but work. She admitted that she was tired and told Scowcroft that she wanted to settle down and maybe start a family. "I felt that it's hard to keep an academic career intact if you don't come back in about two years," Rice later commented. "I think of myself as an academic first… I wanted a life."[54] She also wanted to share her government experiences with her students. She told reporters that she missed the peace of mind that academia afforded her.

President George H.W. Bush praised Rice for her contributions and wished her well. He later wrote:

Condi was brilliant, but she never tried to flaunt it while in meetings with foreign leaders… She had an amazing way of getting along with people, of making a strong point without being disagreeable... She had a manner and presence that disarms the biggest of the big shots. Why? Because they know she knows what she is talking about.[55]

In addition to participating fully as Bush's advisor, Rice had also, during her tenure in Washington, developed close ties with the entire Bush family. She often visited their compound at Kennebunkport, Maine, as well as the Bush home in Houston, Texas. She would maintain these ties following her return to Stanford.

Chapter 4

Provost Rice Advises the Candidate

Rice, after her two-year leave of absence, returned to Stanford and resumed her professorship. She regaled her students with her stories of being an insider to United States foreign policy. In December 1991 she spoke about this.

> All the assumptions that I started out with as a student of international studies have simply been blown away. The old assumptions—that Europe was permanently divided, that the East-West conflict was a permanent fixture of the international system, that Soviet forces would remain deep in Eastern Europe—no longer hold.[56]

She had witnessed history being made and impressed this upon her students.

Provost Rice

In addition to her professorship, Rice was also asked to serve as a member of Stanford's search committee for a new president for the university. Stanford's provost, the second-highest university official, had recently retired and the school administration was searching for someone to take his place. It was during this period of time that Rice captured the eye of Gerhard Caspar, the man who was ultimately chosen to fill the vacant presidency. President Caspar suggested Rice as provost, saying that he was

Stanford University was Rice's "home" for many years as professor and provost.

"greatly impressed by her academic values, her intellectual range, her eloquence... 'I have come to admire her judgment and persuasiveness.'"[57]

After careful consideration, Rice accepted the challenging post. As provost she would be responsible for 1400 faculty members and more than 14,000 students. She would also be responsible for the $1.5 billion budget. Rice became the youngest person ever to hold the position; every previous provost had been at least sixty—she was thirty-eight. Serving as provost from 1993 to 1999, Rice was the first woman and the first nonwhite person to hold the position.

In accepting the new job, Rice said, "I am honored that President Caspar has placed faith in my judgment and ability to meet Stanford's challenges."[58] The job would require many of the skills that Rice already possessed, as historians Morris and McGann explain: "The job required grit, political savvy, and a sublime degree of self-confidence."[59] In addition to serving as provost, Rice decided that she would also continue to teach a number of graduate courses.

Rice Faces a Huge Deficit

As provost, Rice's number-one responsibility was the school's budget. Stanford had, for years, been operating at a huge deficit, somewhere in the neighborhood of $20 to $40 million. The deficit

The 1989 San Francisco Bay area earthquake caused millions of dollars of damage to the Stanford campus, adding to the huge deficit already in place.

On the Board

After working for the first Bush administration, Rice took positions on several corporate boards, the most notable of which was the Chevron Oil Company. Chevron is a multinational oil company with contacts in more than twenty countries. She was appointed to the Board of Directors in 1991 and served there for ten years. Biographer Felix summarizes her experience: "Her expertise on the states that made up the former Soviet Union made her a valuable asset for Chevron's oil interests in Kazakhstan."[1] Chevron even named a supertanker after Rice. Later, when she joined the second Bush administration, Rice resigned her post due to a conflict of interest.

Because of her expertise and experience in the highest ranks of government, Rice was also valuable to a number of other organizations and companies that did business overseas. She served on the Board of Directors for Trans-America, the sixth-largest insurance company in the United States. Other directorships include: Hewlett-Packard (computers), J.P. Morgan (banking), Rand Corporation (think-tank), and Notre Dame University. She also served a two-year term with the National Endowment for Humanities, a group providing grants to scholars and organizations.

1 Antonia Felix. *Condi: The Condoleezza Rice Story.* New York: New Market Press, 2002, p. 164.

had been heavily impacted by the 1989 San Francisco Bay area earthquake, which caused extensive damage to the campus. The construction costs had added millions to an already enormous budget deficit.

To balance the budget, Rice had to make some hard choices. One of the first things she did was to lay off a large number of administrators and teachers. These actions were broadly criticized, and the firing of a popular Chicano assistant dean resulted in a wave of protests and hunger strikes led by the students. According to the *Los Angeles Times*, some of the layoffs were made more brutal "by the imperious ways she carried them out."[60] Rice later said that the job required this kind of decisive attitude; she repeatedly stated that she couldn't have eliminated the deficit by playing personal favorites or listening to the critics.

Many Stanford administrators and professors were also critical of Rice's style, although they praised her efforts to balance the budget. When questioned about why she didn't consult with the faculty committee before making the cuts, she responded, "I don't do committees."[61] Tony Cox of NPR summarized the end result: "As the school's number-two administrator, she presided over a controversial restructuring of the budget that helped stave off a potentially embarrassing fiscal crisis, but also earned a reputation for being cold and autocratic."[62]

Rice later defended herself by saying, "I always feel bad for the dislocation it causes in peoples' lives. When I had to lay people off, I eased the transition for them in any way I could. But sometimes you have to make difficult decisions and you have to make them stick."[63]

Despite doubts that the deficit could be eradicated so quickly, Rice announced in May 1996 that Stanford was on solid ground. Not only was the budget balanced, but the university now had a $14.5 million surplus and reserve.

"Rice Provided Strong Leadership"

Rice's five-year tenure as provost brought other challenges as well, all of which she overcame with composure and determination, according to her colleagues. These issues included a pending threat of legal action against the university, controversy over affirmative action, lack of student housing, and changes in the curriculum. Journalist Herstein summarizes: "Rice provided strong leadership in handling each of these problems and won the respect of the Stanford population."[64]

One of the most challenging issues during the years in which Rice held the position of provost was the use of affirmative action, the hiring of minorities by use of a quota system based on a percentage of the population. Rice, who herself had benefited from affirmative action in obtaining her professorship, chartered a middle course. While she supported using the action to hire faculty members, she opposed the granting of tenure on the basis of a quota system. She expected all faculty members to achieve and advance on their own merits, just as she herself had. Rice stated that she basically supported affirmative action, but "cautioned against diminishing standards to accomplish the need for diversity."[65]

Another critical issue Rice dealt with was a shortage of housing for graduate students. Prior to her becoming provost, nearly 1,000 graduate students had been unable to find campus housing. Once the budget had been balanced, Rice announced that the university would begin construction on new housing for these students. She was also instrumental in settling a dispute with the federal government. Claiming that Stanford was overcharging for tuition and other services, the government ordered an audit. Rice helped with the audit, ultimately disproving the charges.

The number of female professors at Stanford was quite low. Rice addressed this issue in 1994 by creating the Faculty Incentive Fund to distribute money to finance additional faculty positions. She utilized the money to hire more women and minority teachers, forty-six in total. Rice also created a new core curriculum for incoming freshmen and sophomores called "An Introduction to the Humanities." With updated study plans and group projects, the new program was an immediate success.

Of the many jobs she had held up to this point in time, Rice said that tackling the job of provost was perhaps the toughest of them all. "I've always been a pretty self-confident person," she stated. "But you never know if you're going to quite measure up under those circumstances. It was a great joy two or three years later to see the university, now on this new financial footing, spring back to life in the way that it did."[66]

"An Excellent Role Model"

Despite Rice's busy jobs as both provost and professor, she, nonetheless, also found time to do work outside the university. In 1991, for instance, Governor Pete Wilson of California requested that Rice join a committee that was working on new congressional districts and legislation. Six years later, she was asked to serve on the Federal Advisory Committee on Gender-Integrated Training in the Military, a group dedicated to ensuring that women were treated with respect and equality in the armed services. In addition, Rice participated in the Aspen Strategy Group from 1991 to 1995, researching and advising the government on the role of the United States in the post–cold war world. She served as

The Center for a New Generation

Having watched her parents devote so much of their time to disadvantaged minority youths, Rice wanted to do what she could as well. Her favorite project was the Center for a New Generation, an organization she co-founded with her father and philanthropist Susan Ford. The center provides classes for minority children in grades two through eight and has been immensely successful. The students at the center became an extended family for Rice. She stated: "Those are sort of my kids, all 125 of them."[1]

Per Sonam, a twelve-year-old student at the center, spoke of her own appreciation for the organization: "My grades in school used to be pretty average… I've been coming to CNG for three years. We have a Homework Café, where there are some really smart mentors to help us when we need it… My grades have definitely improved. I used to get C's in math, but now I get A's and B's. And this year I actually passed my writing proficiency test. I don't think I could have done it without CNG. I love it here."[2]

1 Quoted in Antonia Felix. *Condi: The Condoleezza Rice Story.* New York: New Market Press, 2002, p. 160.

2 Quoted in "Center for a New Generation." *Boys and Girls Club of the Peninsula.* www.bgcp.org/cng_programs.php

consultant on Soviet affairs for ABC News in 1991, as well as giving a speech at the 1992 Republican National Convention on behalf of her former employer, George H.W. Bush. She seemed to thrive on all the activity.

While at Stanford, Rice also wrote three books along with more than twenty articles that were published in a variety of academic journals. Her first book was one based on her doctoral dissertation and was entitled *Uncertain Allegiance: The Soviet Union and the Czechoslovak Army,* published in 1984. This was followed by *The Gorbachev Era* in 1986 and *Germany Unified and Europe Transformed* with Philip Zelikow in 1995. The latter book was about her years in the Bush administration, including the reunification of Germany and the fall of the Soviet Union.

Rice also received outside recognition for her efforts while at Stanford. In 1992, for instance, the California Women's Legislator's Caucus named Rice their "Woman of the Year." State Senator Becky Morgan stated, "Dr. Rice has participated in the making of history. Condoleezza exemplifies everything that a woman can be: intelligent, articulate, capable, and highly respected. She is an excellent role model for younger women."[67] Five years later, she was elected to the American Academy of Arts and Sciences, an honor given to those who make significant contributions to those fields.

"I'm Going to Take a Leave"

Despite her love of teaching and her satisfaction with being provost, toward the end of 1998 Rice made a difficult decision. She told university officials that she was anxious to return to hands-on foreign policy and would be taking a leave of absence from Stanford. She announced that she was going to take a position at the Hoover Institution, where she planned on utilizing her international relations experience to advise multinational corporations and other groups.

President Gerhard Caspar, in an official ceremony, thanked Rice for all her many contributions to Stanford, commenting that she had invested "as much talent and energy into consolidating the Stanford budget as into unifying Germany."[68] He presented her with a rare six-volume edition of Leo Tolstoy's *War and Peace*. The dedication read: "To Condoleezza Rice. May War be the fiction and Peace the reality. With the greatest appreciation and deep gratitude for her service as Stanford's 9th provost."[69]

Rice officially stepped down on July 1, 1999. Upon her arrival at the Hoover Institution, director John Raisian welcomed her warmly, "What we're trying to do is generate ideas that will make the world a little better place, a safer place... This is right up her alley and what she does... She will become an integral part of Hoover's foreign policy outlook."[70]

A Meeting with the Candidate

During the years in which she served as provost, Rice had maintained friendly ties with former President Bush and his family. During a visit to his Texas home, the former president asked Rice to meet with his son, George W. Bush, then governor of Texas. She traveled to Austin, Texas, in 1995 for a meeting with Bush, who was, at that time, considering a run for the presidency in 2000. It was not their first introduction, but it was the first time the two had met one-on-one.

The get-together in Austin was the beginning of a long-term relationship and friendship between Rice and Bush based on mutual respect and admiration. In part, the attraction was based on their love of sports—Rice with her knowledge of professional football and Bush with his love of baseball. He had been, at one time, the owner of the Texas Rangers baseball team. Their relationship, however, was based even more on their similar views about America's position in the world, along with their shared belief in God. Morris and McGann elaborate:

> It seems to have been Rice's spiritual heritage that did more than anything else to build the relationship. Their shared commitment to injecting spiritual concerns into their public policy work animated the relationship and made it closer.[71]

In 1998, Bush and Rice met again, this time at the Bush compound in Kennebunkport, Maine. Governor Bush was preparing to announce his candidacy for president. During their visit in Maine, Bush and Rice had a series of intense conversations about global issues and foreign policy. Historian Mann elaborates:

> Over a few days, the son of a former president and the protégé of the former national security advisor [Scowcroft] tested each other. They went fishing and worked out together on the treadmills, bikes, and rowing machines at the Kennebunkport compound.[72]

Historian and journalist Bob Woodward further elaborates: "His [Bush's] questions flowed all weekend—what about this country, this leader, this issue, what might it mean, and what was the angle for United States policy?"[73]

Having little to no experience with foreign policy, Bush relied heavily on Rice, who educated him on international relations. Bush described Rice as "someone who can explain to me foreign policy matters in a way I can understand."[74]

"A Man of Uncommonly Good Judgment"

In addition to tutoring Bush on the intricacies of foreign policy, Rice was also very vocal in her support of him during the 2000 presidential campaign. In an article in *Foreign Affairs,* for instance, Rice wrote about the need to refocus American foreign policy in the absence of cold war tensions. She wrote: "During these fluid times, one can affect the shape of the world to come."[75] She then proceeded to set forth several major priorities: making sure the American armed forces could deter war and defend the country as needed; promoting economic growth; renewing strong relationships with America's allies; and dealing decisively with rogue regimes. Many political insiders believed the Rice article to be an unofficial statement of Bush's own foreign policy agenda.

Later, in August 2000, Rice gave a speech at the Republican National Convention in support of Bush.

In August 2000 Rice spoke at the Republican National Convention in support of George W. Bush.

... George W. Bush, the George W. Bush that I know, is a man of uncommonly good judgment. He is focused and consistent. He believes that we Americans are at our best when we exercise power without fanfare and arrogance. He speaks plainly and with a positive spirit.[76]

Rice served not only as Bush's tutor and advisor but also played an important role in the campaign. She was an integral part of "Women for W" and, as an African American, was essential in garnering black votes. After a close and controversial election, Bush emerged victorious. Even before the results came in, there was little doubt in anyone's mind that Bush would give Rice a prominent position in his new administration. Jay Nordlinger

Rice Tutors Bush

In late 1999, after George W. Bush had announced that he was running for president, he called upon Rice to be his primary foreign policy advisor and tutor. Rice put together a number of half-day training seminars for Bush. She and others presented such topics as national defense, military affairs, and weapons proliferation. Since Bush didn't like to read prepared material, Rice set up numerous question-and-answer sessions for him. He would ask questions, while she and others would answer.

She also spent many hours with Bush prior to each of the presidential debates, peppering him with possible questions he might be asked. Bush has repeatedly credited Rice with enabling him to make a good impression in the televised programs.

in the *National Review,* in fact, predicted that "whatever post Condoleezza Rice received in the administration, she would be 'rock-star' big—a household name."[77]

Chapter 5

National Security Advisor

On December 18, 2000, President-elect George W. Bush announced that Rice would be his National Security Advisor. As such, she would become the first woman in American history to be named to this position. In his comments, Bush stated: "Dr. Rice is not only a brilliant person, she is an experienced person. She is a good manager. I trust her judgment."[78]

As National Security Advisor, Rice would chair the Principals Committee, a group consisting of the Secretaries of State and Defense, as well as the CIA director, the Vice President, and the Chairman of the Joint Chiefs of Staff. Journalist Elizabeth Bumiller describes the importance of Rice's new job:

> The National Security Advisor is a key position, no matter who is in the White House. Generally, he or she is involved in all foreign policy matters, coordinating the work of the Defense and State departments and intelligence agencies like the CIA—and often refereeing among these powerful players when they have conflicting advice for the president.[79]

"Condi Will Report to Me"

On January 22, 2001, Rice was sworn in as National Security Advisor. A few days later, she attended the first Principals meeting. Before discussing any issues, the president made an announcement: "Condi will run these meetings. I'll be seeing all of you regularly, but I want you to debate things out here and then Condi will report to me."[80] Rice's friendship with Bush, along with the confidence that the president had in her, helped consolidate her position as perhaps one of the two most trusted confidants of the president, with Vice President Richard Cheney being the other.

Rice's and Bush's beliefs and world vision complimented each other, producing an effective working partnership. Evan Thomas, writing for *Newsweek*, wrote about their relationship:

> Superficially Bush and Rice are opposites: the rich white boy from Texas who goofed off in school; the middle-class black girl who was a grind. But in fact, they are well matched … the two are possessed of a certain defiant independence,

The Bush Doctrine

During the first term of the Bush administration, the president and his advisors embarked on a new course in foreign policy. Called the Bush Doctrine, the policy centered around the United States acting alone when necessary to protect American interests. Rice fully supported the idea of one power, namely the United States, leading the way for the rest of the world. A key to this new doctrine was the concept of invading or attacking countries that posed potential threats to the United States.

In talking about the Bush Doctrine, Rice has stated that the United States would act in any way necessary to defeat terrorism, including an attack on any country that hid or helped terrorists. The policy asserted that the United States had the right to take such action against any state believed to be a threat to American national interests. Rice states: "The United States has always reserved the right to try and diminish or to try to eliminate a threat before it is attacked."[1]

1 Quoted in "Profile: Condoleezza Rice." *BBC News*, March 30, 2006. http://news.bbc. co.uk/2/hi/americas/3609327.stm

almost an orneriness. They know what it's like to be under-estimated, and they take obvious pleasure in going their own way.[81]

Historians Morris and McGann agree with this assessment and conclude:

> President Bush is a person of instinct, gut, and impulse; his views on foreign policy stem, in large part, from his sense of right and wrong. Rice, by contrast, is a skilled academic, used to assessing evidence dispassionately and applying scientific method to public policy analysis.[82]

Despite Rice's complimentary partnership with Bush, many political insiders questioned whether Rice's relative youth and inexperience at the highest levels of politics would hinder her effectiveness. Many prominent politicians, as a result, attempted to intimidate Rice. Former CIA Chief and current Secretary of Defense Robert Gates remembered an occasion when a treasury department official tried to undermine her authority: "With a smile on her face, she sliced and diced him."[83] Rice has been more than successful, according to political analysts, in holding her own and setting forth her own agenda in the Bush administration than many political experts expected.

Early Challenges

Rice's first eight months as National Security Advisor were busy ones as she studied and dealt with the issues of the day. Almost immediately, she was embroiled in settling a significant crisis with China. An American reconnaissance plane had collided with a Chinese aircraft and been forced to make a landing in Chinese territory. The Chinese government refused to release the crew until the United States made a public apology for violating their airspace. Rice advised the president to do just that and the tense situation was eventually resolved in a peaceful manner.

For the first time in her career, Rice had successfully dealt with a country other than the Soviet Union. In talking of the Chinese

Soon after she became National Security Advisor, Rice was tested with a crisis involving China and the crew of an American reconnaissance plane. She successfully brought the crew home.

crisis and other potential problems, she freely admitted: "I've been pressed to understand parts of the world that have not really been part of my scope." She then added: "The threat of biological and chemical weapons is fast and growing ... [such threats] can come from small states and terrorists just as easily as one powerful adversary."[84]

September 11, 2001

Those words took on new meaning on the morning of September 11, 2001. As was her usual routine, Rice was in her office at 6:30 A.M. While doing work at her desk, she was interrupted by her secretary who told Rice that a plane had just hit the World Trade Center at 8:45 A.M. She immediately called President

On September 11, 2001, a crisis of great magnitude occurred when terrorists attacked the World Trade Center.

Bush, who was speaking in Florida; they both believed initially that the crash was an accident. After a second plane hit the Trade Center, there was no doubt, however, that it was an attack. Once again, Rice notified Bush and then immediately called a meeting for the top members of the National Security Council. Shortly thereafter she learned of a similar attack on the Pentagon and an aborted attack on the White House that resulted in a crash in rural Pennsylvania.

As the White House was being evacuated, Rice and her team moved to an underground bunker. She and Vice President Cheney talked again with President Bush and advised him not to return to Washington until the military was certain the attacks were over. Bush would spend the day flying from military base to military base before returning that evening to the White House.

Rice's next calls were placed to various foreign heads of state to notify them that the American government was still intact and operational. She stayed in contact with the president throughout the day, notifying him of each significant occurrence. While obviously disturbed and concerned about what had happened, Rice said later that her faith kept her strong: "Since I was a girl I have relied on faith—a belief that I'm never alone … that has always been a part of me, and I'm drawing on that now."[85]

"Giving the President the Whole Story"

In the days following the terrorist attacks, Rice became one of the most visible of Bush's representatives. She made numerous appearances on television, giving press conferences and updates on the government's response to the atrocities. She talked daily with both Secretary of Defense Donald Rumsfeld and Secretary of State Colin Powell. Her job was to gather information from the various members of the Principals Committee and then present each view to the president. "I try very hard to remember that I have to be very disciplined about making sure I'm giving the president the whole story," she told reporters, "that I'm making sure he knows everything."[86]

A Fitness Freak

During her work in government, as well as during her college years, Rice maintained her physical health by participating in a strenuous fitness program. Rice and her trainers developed a rigorous workout that included the treadmill, stretching, and weights. Mark Mateska, a trainer for Rice, stated: "I put her through the same regime I did with any athlete at Stanford. She felt that her workouts kept her sharp physically, as well as mentally."[1] Rice reported that the workouts helped control the stress in her busy, complex life.

Since moving to Washington, Rice has spoken frequently of her need for fitness: "Athletics gives you a kind of toughness and discipline that nothing else really does."[2] Rice has always believed that by working out she was becoming stronger and more disciplined. During her years in the White House, she has often worked out with the president, who shares her belief in the need for physical fitness.

Fitness training, Rice believes, keeps her sharp and controls the stress.

1 Quoted in Antonia Felix. *Condi: The Condoleezza Rice Story*. New York: New Market Press, 2002, p. 185.

2 Quoted in Felix. *Condi: The Condoleezza Rice Story*, p. 84.

Prior to September 11, the National Security Council generally met only twice a month; in the days afterwards, it met three times a week. In the first few months following the attacks, Rice and the other advisors dealt with immense challenges. The perpetrators of the events of September 11 were quickly identified as members of al-Qaeda, an Islamist terrorist group responsible for earlier attacks against American embassies in Africa. Once this had been determined, the council focused on the search for al-Qaeda leader Osama bin Laden, the threat of more attacks, and the anthrax crisis. The latter crisis resulted from the discovery of the anthrax virus in mail delivered to prominent newspeople along with government representatives. A number of individuals died as a result of their exposure. The council considered future anthrax attacks as a significant threat to Americans.

Rice was a key member of the president's team that explored what the best response to the 9/11 attacks would be. She strongly supported President Bush's decision to invade Afghanistan and attack the al-Qaeda strongholds there. She was also the person who tried to soften the impact on the Afghani people by creating a food drop to tell the people that the United States was not at war with them, but rather with the terrorists who had found a haven in their country. The Taliban, an al-Qaeda-influenced group that had been ruling Afghanistan, was defeated in five weeks, but bin Laden was not found.

The Fallout from 9/11

Almost immediately following the terrorist attacks, controversy arose as to how much the president and his advisors knew about the al-Qaeda threat prior to September 11. One of the strongest critics of the Bush administration was Richard A. Clarke, the former head of the Counter-Terrorism section of the National Security Council. He was one of the first witnesses called by the 9/11 Commission, an independent group of prominent lawyers and politicians, formed to investigate the tragedy. The group was created by Congress and the members then appointed by President Bush in late 2002. Over a two-year period, the commission heard testimony from Bush administration representatives, as well as members of the CIA, FBI, and other intelligence agencies. After two years of deliberation, the commission published a lengthy and complex report, concluding that many factors led to the 9/11 attacks, the primary one being a lack of cooperation and coordination between intelligence agencies.

Clarke, in testimony before the 9/11 Commission, reported that he had repeatedly voiced his concerns about the growth of

Rice's Faith Keeps her Strong

Condoleezza Rice's faith has always been an important part of her life and has provided motivation for her to succeed and advance in her endeavors. "I'm a really religious person," she explained. "That faith has manifested itself as a respect for family traditions, love for children, love for music and the arts, love and service for her country, and hope for a peaceful world."[1]

Rice has also spoken of how her faith keeps her optimistic: "I don't believe that I was put on this earth to be sour, so I'm eternally optimistic about things."[2]

Journalist Jim Puzzanghera elaborates on this theme of optimism: "Rice is fond of saying she approaches life with no grand plan, leaping from one opportunity to the next, guided by a deep belief in God that she is headed in the right direction."[3] This optimism and faith proved invaluable to her in the weeks after 9/11.

Rice used prayer frequently in the days following the attacks and has continued to do so before making important foreign policy decisions as well. "Prayer is very important to me," she states. "And a belief that if you ask for it, you will be guided…"[4]

With George Bush, Rice shares a deep belief and faith in God.

1 Quoted in Arthur Herstein. "Acorns to Oaks." *World and I*, August 1, 2004.

2 Quoted in Antonia Felix. *Condi: The Condoleezza Rice Story*. New York: New Market Press, 2002, p. 3.

3 Jim Puzzanghera. "Condoleezza Rice Returns to Stanford." *Knight Ridder/Tribune News Service*, June 15, 2002.

4 Quoted in Dick Morris and Eileen McGann. *Condi vs. Hillary: The Next Great Presidential Race*. New York: Regan Books, 2005, p. 131.

al-Qaeda. He stated that during that time he had sent numerous reports to Rice, in particular a note on August 6, 2001, that advised the administration that al-Qaeda was planning to hijack airliners and attack the United States.

Clarke then charged that Rice and others in the administration had largely dismissed the memo, claiming that if an attack occurred at all, it would be on foreign soil. In his testimony, Clarke repeatedly accused Bush's national security advisors, and Rice in particular, of having failed to take his warnings of al-Qaeda attacks on America seriously.

Other criticism came from many of the families of 9/11's victims. Stephen Push, who represented the families in testifying, stated:

> I was disappointed that Dr. Rice didn't take responsibility for what happened on her watch, spent a lot of time trying to pass blame off on others, and never really acknowledged that there were serious problems in the intelligence community prior to 9/11 that need to be addressed.[87]

Despite these criticisms, Rice repeatedly stated that the administration did everything it could have done prior to the attacks. In her testimony before the 9/11 Commission she said, "I don't remember the al-Qaeda cells as being something we were told we needed to do something about."[88] Rice also dismissed the importance of Clarke's August memo, stating that it had not specified any threats inside the United States. Many of Rice's critics, however, continue to believe that she failed, as National Security Advisor, in passing on critical information to the president on this issue.

Invasion

After the attacks of September 11 and the victories in Afghanistan, the focus of Rice and the Bush administration continued to be on the worldwide fight against terrorism. Rice had already identified the danger posed by small states and terrorists in earlier speeches. During 2002, she and other Bush advisors sought to find the proper response to this growing threat. Looking to expand the fight against terrorism, Rice therefore encouraged the president to focus on those countries that sponsored terrorism. Three nations were pinpointed. The countries were identified in President Bush's State of the Union address given in January 2002. Iraq, Iran, and North Korea were identified as "Axis of Evil" countries; these nations were considered to be the primary sponsors of terrorism.

Focusing on these countries toward the end of 2002, the Bush administration turned first to Iraq and brought attention to the nation's repeated failure to comply with United Nations resolutions

Rice believed that there were links between Saddam Hussein, leader of Iraq, and al-Qaeda.

to destroy their weapons, especially those of mass destruction, such as nuclear and chemical weapons. Rice addressed this issue in an article, which appeared in the *New York Times* on January 23, 2002. She wrote: "By both its actions and its inactions, Iraq is proving not that it is a nation bent on disarmament, but that it is a nation with something to hide… It should know that time is running out."[89] Later Rice would add: "… there will always … be some uncertainty about how quickly he [Iraqi leader Saddam Hussein] can acquire nuclear weapons. But we don't want the smoking gun to be a mushroom cloud."[90]

Rice, in preparing her advice to the president, had numerous meetings with Hans Blix, the United Nations official in charge of monitoring Iraq's disarmament. Blix believed that Iraq was hiding weapons of mass destruction and shared the latest information with Rice. Based on this information and other reports from the intelligence community, Rice told the president that she did not believe that Saddam Hussein would comply with the United Nations resolution.

In addition to the accusations about Iraq having weapons of mass destruction, the Bush administration, based on reports from the intelligence community, also asserted that there were ties between Hussein and al-Qaeda. Rice spoke for the president when she stated in early 2003 on the CBS program *Face the Nation*: "Now the al-Qaeda is an organization that's quite dispersed—and quite widespread in its effects, but it clearly has had links to the Iraqis."[91] Despite this claim, no documentation was ever produced proving that this was true, nor were any weapons of mass destruction ever discovered. Critics later censured the administration for making decisions based on erroneous and, in some cases, falsified information.

Iraq Strategy

After listening to advice from Rice and others, Bush made the decision to invade Iraq on March 19, 2003. In the months following this decision, Rice staunchly defended the president, stating that only after all other choices had been explored was the decision for war made. Military action in Iraq led to the defeat of the Iraqi army and the eventual capture of Hussein in December 2003, along with what the president referred to as the liberation of the Iraqi people. In a speech given in Los Angeles on June 12, 2003, Rice stated, "In Iraq, a murderous tyrant and a supporter of terror has been defeated, and a free society is rising... The transition from dictatorship to democracy will take time, but it is worth the effort."[92]

While the announcement of victory had been quick, the situation in Iraq soon deteriorated. Making peace was proving to be a difficult task. In early 2004, President Bush turned over much of the planning and post-war policy decisions to Rice and the National Security Council. Unhappy with the Department of Defense's failure to deal with the increasing insurgency in Iraq, Bush asked Rice to coordinate with the Coalition Provisional Authority, a temporary Iraqi government that would eventually be replaced by democratically elected officials. Rice, as head of the Iraq Stabilization Group, told reporters that the group's goal was to work with the provisional government to help smooth the way to the ultimate transition to a democratic Iraqi government. Nicholas Lemman of Columbia University spoke of Rice's qualifications for this job: "Rice is a superb administrator... She is ... someone you can turn to and say ... 'Make sure everything is buttoned down. If tough, harsh things need to be done, do them.' She's absolutely not hesitant about doing that stuff."[93] Rice pledged to bring the right kinds of people together to achieve a successful transition. Despite her promise, however, the situation in Iraq did not improve. American military deaths increased as new waves of violence broke out throughout the country. Rice and other American officials were later criticized for their failure to stabilize the situation in Iraq. Lemman, for instance, stated that while "Rice is a superb administrator ... she is not an expert on the Middle East or on social reconstruction efforts."[94]

Was Rice Effective?

With the end of Bush's first term in office and the presidential elections of 2004 fast approaching, the press and the American public began analyzing Rice's effectiveness as National Security Advisor. Many politicians and analysts criticized Rice's support of the Iraq war. They charged that there had been little planning for post-war Iraq and also pointed to the fact that bin Laden had not been captured. Peter Slevin of the *Washington Post* addressed this: "Frankly, she's run into some criticism increasingly since the war for running an NSC that does not, in fact, ride hard very well on the different agencies, that she seeks to build consensus but has not always … been tough enough in carrying out those duties."[95]

Despite the criticism, Rice had remained popular and received high approval ratings from the American public. Rice, the public felt, had done a good job of mediating between powerful voices in the Bush administration. Analysts also pointed out that it was Rice who had helped the president reach decisions when he received conflicting advice from Secretary of State Colin Powell and Secretary of Defense Donald Rumsfeld. Biographer Felix gives her opinion: "[Rice] has run a tight ship, keeping the egos at bay as the administration works through one crisis to the next."[96]

Campaigning for Bush

In addition to her continuing duties, in late 2003 and 2004, Rice also became the first National Security Advisor to campaign actively for a candidate during a presidential election. As an active campaign speaker, Rice reiterated the importance of continuing the fight against terrorism. "To win the war on terror, we must also win a war of ideas by appealing to the decent hopes of people throughout the world," she stated in a speech in 2003. "Power in the service of freedom is to be welcomed, and powers that share a commitment to freedom can, and must, make common cause against freedom's enemies."[97]

With Rice's help, President George W. Bush defeated Senator John Kerry in a close election. There were many critical issues that would need to be addressed in Bush's next term and the president vowed to make some necessary changes in his administration. Rice would soon find herself playing a new and more powerful role.

Chapter 6

Madam Secretary

In November 2004 following President Bush's re-election, Secretary of State Colin Powell announced that he was retiring from his position. Shortly thereafter, President Bush nominated his National Security Advisor, Condoleezza Rice, as Powell's

Rice was sworn in as Secretary of State on January 26, 2005, after the retirement of Colin Powell.

73

successor. In making the announcement, the president stated: "During the last four years, I've relied on her counsel, benefited from her great experience, and appreciated her sound and steady judgment… The Secretary of State is America's face to the world, and in Dr. Rice the world will see the strength, the grace, and decency of our country."[98]

The Confirmation Hearings

Before Rice took over the State Department, she first faced confirmation hearings in the Senate. During the hearings, several Senators voiced skepticism about her nomination. Senator Robert Byrd of Virginia, for instance, explained his reservations and charged her with failing to protect the United States from the September 11 attacks. He also criticized her unwavering support of the invasion of Iraq.

Going a step further, Senator Barbara Boxer, a long-time critic of the Bush administration, accused Rice of untruthfulness: "Your loyalty to the mission you were given to sell this war overwhelmed your respect for the truth." Rice angrily responded: "Senator, I have to say that I have never, ever lost respect for the truth in the service of anything."[99]

However, Senator Joe Lieberman, former Democratic candidate for Vice President, supported Rice's nomination. In a statement he offered words of appreciation for her experience:

I conclude that Dr. Condoleezza Rice is uniquely prepared by ability and experience to lead this effort as Secretary of State… President Bush has clearly nominated Dr. Rice … because he values her experience, he knows her skill and he trusts her counsel… She has earned the nomination that the President has just given her… Now she can, and I believe will, help lead our nation to change the world and in doing so to advance our values and protect our security for our children and grandchildren as well.[100]

During Rice's own testimony before the committee, she answered her critics, denying the charges that she had been untruthful and telling the senators that she and the Bush administration had

Secretary of State

The position of Secretary of State was created in 1789 by the first Congress. The Secretary of State is the president's chief foreign affairs advisor and carries out the president's policies through the workings of the State Department and the Foreign Service, including ambassadors to foreign nations and other diplomats. It is up to the Secretary of State to conduct negotiations with other foreign leaders, as well as hammering out treaties and other agreements. The State Department also ensures the safety and protection of American citizens who are traveling abroad; to do this, the State Department has a file of countries that it deems "not safe" for American travel. It is also the Secretary of State's responsibility to report directly to Congress and the American public about the conduct of foreign relations.

When Rice was National Security Advisor, she met with the other major department heads in government and then took their recommendations back to the president. She advised the president directly on the best course of foreign policy action to take based on this input from others. As Secretary of State, however, Rice's main responsibility is to the State Department. In this role, she became a diplomat, meeting with foreign leaders to work on world solutions through diplomacy. While she remains one of the president's closest advisors, Rice does not, as Secretary of State, coordinate between the other offices.

Thomas Jefferson was the first Secretary of State.

THOMAS JEFFERSON.

done everything in their power to protect the American people. She also stressed the need for further diplomacy in dealing with terrorism, stating:

> Under the vision and leadership of President Bush, our nation has risen to meet the challenges of our time, fighting tyranny and terror and securing the blessings of freedom and prosperity for a new generation... Now it is the time to build on these achievements to make the world safer and to make the world more free. We must use American diplomacy to help create a balance of power in the world that favors freedom. The time for diplomacy is now.[101]

The Senate ultimately voted to approve Rice's nomination by a vote of 85 to 13. The thirteen negative votes were the largest number in American history to be cast against a nominee. She became the 66th Secretary of State on January 26, 2005.

Independent Secretary or Presidential Mouthpiece?

The confirmation hearings raised some interesting questions. Always been a staunch defender of the Bush administration and its policies, many politicians and journalists were skeptical as to whether Rice could function independently.

Elaine Shannon, a *Time* magazine State Department correspondent, spoke about this concern on a radio program.

> Condoleezza Rice seems to be a very proud woman, a very intelligent woman, a woman who's going to stand her ground... But she's always going to be very much part of George W. Bush's inner circle and I don't think she's going to ever say anything that would cast him in a bad light.[102]

Other journalists and analysts also questioned Rice's effectiveness. Leslie Gelb, president of the Council on Foreign Relations asserted: "She's perceived as an extension of President Bush ... so I think she will be regarded by most of her counterparts around the world with some suspicion and wariness."[103] The *Miami Herald* was one of many newspapers and magazines in which editorials voiced skepticism: "In Rice, Bush nominates a friend to lead the State Department. Bush apparently wants to end internal bickering and ensure that the administration speaks with one voice on foreign-policy issues."[104]

One of Rice's former students, protégées, and friend, Kiron Skinner (a professor at Carnegie Mellon University, Pittsburgh, Pennsylvania), however, believes that Rice could and would be independent. In an interview, Skinner reported: "If one knows Rice, and I've known her now for about twenty years, the first thing that jumps out is that she's fiercely independent as a person and in terms of her character and in terms of her intellect, and I believe that both will come to the fore now that she will be the chief spokesperson and diplomat and America's face to the world."[105]

Rice and the Ongoing Fight Against Terrorism

As America's primary diplomat and spokesperson, Rice has had to contend with multiple problems and issues. One of the most important of these issues has been the ongoing fight to end

In 2004, Afghanis stood in long lines for hours for the privilege of voting for the first time.

terrorism at home and abroad. Rice believes that the United States is winning that war. At an American Legion Convention on August 29, 2006, Rice spoke on this issue:

> Consider the progress we have made: Five years ago, the members of al-Qaeda were largely free to operate, to organize, to travel, to move money, to communicate with each other, and to plan attacks to murder innocent people. Today, however, five years later, America is leading a great coalition of countries in the fight against terrorists. Together, we are seizing their money. We're closing their sanctuaries. We're hunting their cells. We're killing and capturing their leaders. Ladies and gentlemen: We are waging a global war on terrorism, and we are breaking the back of the al-Qaeda network.[106]

As part of the fight against terrorism, the Bush administration has promoted the need for democratic change in the Middle East and elsewhere. In a speech at the Institute for Political Studies in Paris, France, in early 2005, Rice stated the administration's position:

> In Afghanistan just a few months ago, men and women once suppressed by the Taliban, walked miles, forded streams, and stood hours in the snow just to cast a ballot for their first vote as a free people. And just a few days ago in Iraq, millions of Iraqi men and women defied the terrorist threats and delivered a clarion call for freedom... They cast their free votes and began their nation's new history... In our time we have an historic opportunity to shape a global balance of power that favors freedom... We must build on recent successes by stabilizing and advancing democratic progress in Afghanistan and Iraq... We know we have to deal with the world as it is. But we do not have to accept the world as it is.[107]

Rice's Focus on Iraq

As part of the ongoing war on terrorism, Rice, in her new position as Secretary of State, needed to focus much of her attention on the deteriorating situation in Iraq. Terrorists and

Rice has been to Iraq many times.

other groups opposed to American involvement in the Middle East had increased their violence, and the death toll for both American military personnel and Iraqi civilians continued to rise.

To deal with the problems in Iraq, Rice needed first-hand information. Prior to becoming Secretary, Rice had visited Iraq only once. She decided to remedy this almost immediately. She traveled to Iraq in May 2005 and spent time visiting military hospitals and meeting with the Iraqi prime minister and others in the Iraqi government.

For the first time, Rice was personally seeing the effects of the war on the American military. She later stated: "I have to be able to look at these young soldiers and ask myself honestly if I think what they're going through was worth it, and are we making it worth it."[108] Despite being emotionally affected by the devastation she witnessed, Rice maintains that the war is still essential and that bringing democracy to the Middle East is supremely

The Palestinian–Israeli Conflict

A major issue that Secretary of State Rice dealt with was the ongoing Palestinian–Israeli conflict. Continuing hostilities and clashes between rival factions in Palestine, however, threatened any kind of resolution. Most political analysts agree that this violence could engulf the entire region in chaos and undermine the Palestinian leadership. Whether Rice and the Bush administration were ultimately successful in brokering a peace agreement remained to be seen.

The violence in Palestine and Israel threatens the entire Middle East, so a peace agreement between the two countries is crucial.

As of 2007, the Bush administration supported a program to create an independent Palestine that comprised territory in the Gaza Strip and West Bank areas. For this plan to be successful, however, there would have to be concessions on both sides. Rice, as Secretary of State, was very active in the peace process. For instance, she was in the Middle East to meet with the Israelis and Palestinians in mid-January 2007. After a meeting with Palestinian Prime Minister Mahmoud Abbas, Rice stated: "I have heard loud and clear the call for deeper American engagement in these processes. You will have my commitment to do precisely that... I'm going to enlist the support of anybody I can to try and move forward a Palestinian state living at peace side by side with Israel. That is the goal here."[1]

1 Quoted in Anne Gearan. "Rice Says She Registers Mideast Demands." Associated Press, January 14, 2007. http://news.yaho.com/s/ap/20070114/ap_on_re_mid_ea.rice

important. Since that time, she has made numerous trips to Iraq as she continues to work with the Iraqi government.

Rice continues to support the American presence in Iraq. In a speech to the American Legion on August 29, 2006, Rice stated:

> Most Iraqis want what all people want. They want freedom from coercion and oppression, safety from violence and injustice, opportunities for a better life for themselves and for their children… I submit to you that if we stay strong, if we stay committed, if we remain true to our values, that one day, people will look back and they will say, 'Who could ever have doubted that … the universal values of democracy and freedom would take hold in the Middle East?' … and they will say 'Thank God that America stayed the course.'[109]

Faced with increased violence from opponents of the new Iraqi government and American intervention, on January 10, 2007, President Bush announced that the United States would be sending more troops to Iraq in an effort to curb the insurgency and hasten the American withdrawal from that country. It was a very unpopular announcement with both the public and congressional members, many of whom were becoming more and more critical of the war itself and the continued presence of American troops in Iraq. In the days following the president's decision, Secretary Rice was in the news frequently as she defended the troop increase and the president's action.

Rice Watches Iran Closely

In addition to dealing with the war in Iraq, Secretary Rice has also had to contend with a growing nuclear threat in Iran. In recent years, Iran has heavily promoted its nuclear research and uranium enrichment programs. While Iran maintains that these programs will be used strictly for civilian energy, Rice and President Bush believe otherwise, as do many other foreign leaders. Because of Iran's long history of supporting terrorism, Rice believes that Iranian nuclear capability threatens the safety of the entire Middle East and the world in general.

As a result of her concerns, on July 12, 2006, Rice joined the foreign ministers of China, Russia, Great Britain, Germany, France, and the European Union in announcing that those nations would seek a United Nations resolution demanding that Iran stop its nuclear program. The crisis with Iran is a continuing one that may not be resolved in the near future. In the meantime, Rice, as Secretary of State, stays incommunication with other diplomats and watches Iran closely, looking for any evidence of aggression.

In addition to the nuclear threat, Rice has also called Iran one of the world's largest supporters of terrorism and has condemned the support that Iran gives to the insurgency in Iraq. In testimony before the Senate Budget Committee in February 2006, Rice accused "… [Iran] of being the central banker for terrorism around the world and working with Syria to destabilize the Middle East."[110]

Rice and North Korea

Rice has also identified North Korea as being part of the "Axis of Evil." One of her biggest concerns, as with Iran, has been North Korea's possession of nuclear weapons. This concern centered on the possibility that North Korea would develop the potential to attack the United States and its allies with nuclear warheads.

Because of these concerns, Rice led a series of negotiations, called the Six-Party talks, that included representatives from six nations—China, North Korea, South Korea, Russia, Japan, and the United States. The purpose of the talks was to persuade North Korea to stop its nuclear program. However, the talks failed to produce a disarmament.

In 2006, North Korea test-fired seven rockets with nuclear warheads, earning international condemnation. And on October 9, 2006, North Korea tested its first nuclear explosive device. Afterward, Rice and the other members of the Six-Party talks, with North Korea not present, worked with the United Nations Security Council to pass a resolution against North Korea.

The resolution contained language demanding that North Korea destroy all its nuclear weapons.

Since that time, Rice has continued to work toward reopening talks with North Korea. In mid-February 2007, Rice's hard work paid off when North Korea announced that it would disarm. As of June 2007, details on the disarmament still had to be worked out, but Rice felt optimistic that this move would lessen tensions between the United States and North Korea.

The State Department

With crises to deal with in Iraq, Iran, and North Korea, Rice has been an incredibly active Secretary of State. In addition to dealing with those countries, one of her biggest tasks has been to repair the damage that has been done to America's relationships with European nations. Tensions have remained high between the United States and these countries over the invasion of Iraq, the treatment of the terror suspects, and many of the moves made by the Bush Administration without the approval of foreign allies. Relying on face-to-face diplomacy with foreign leaders across the world, Rice has been tireless in her efforts to repair America's image.

Since assuming her position as Secretary of State, Rice has also taken measures to reform and restructure the State Department. She refers to this plan as "Transformational Diplomacy" and describes it as a way to "work with our many partners around the world ... build and sustain democratic, well-governed states that will respond to the needs of their people and conduct themselves responsibly in the international system."[111] The plan has met with overall support from the national and international communities.

Rice announced that there were several core elements to this new kind of diplomacy. The first is to relocate many of America's diplomats and ambassadors to places in the world where they are needed most, such as Iraq, Afghanistan, and the Serbian states. Along with this relocation, all diplomats would rotate their positions so that everyone would serve a tour of duty in these hardship areas. Rice also recommends that diplomats be able to speak at least two other languages besides English in conflict areas.

Another core element of Transformational Diplomacy will involve finding solutions to regional problems rather than focusing on international issues. The problems to be addressed on a regional basis include such issues as terrorism, drug-trafficking, and health care. While terrorism and drugs are international issues, Rice hopes that, by working on a country-to-country basis, these problems can be eliminated at the source. Rice also envisions the United States working with nations around the world to help them build stronger governments, and, in the process, decreasing foreign dependence on American assistance.

Rice sees these new initiatives as important for American foreign policy in the future. She believes that in strengthening these individual governments and eradicating the need for outside support, there will be less temptation for those countries to be overtaken by terrorist regimes. She compares this kind of diplomacy to the steps taken after World War II to help stabilize Western Europe in the face of communism. By supporting former allies, the United States was able to prevent communist takeovers of those areas.

Rice has further stated that her goal in this area is

> to work with our many partners around the world to build and sustain democratic, well-governed states that will respond to the needs of their people... Transformational democracy is rooted in partnership, not paternalism—in doing things with other people, not for them.[112]

High Approval Ratings

With Rice's new policy being viewed as a positive step toward better diplomacy abroad, her popularity ratings remained high, despite President Bush's approval ratings being at an all-time low. More than two-thirds of the public say that she is doing a good job. Journalist Jonathan Beale from the BBC writes about the job she has done:

> There is no doubt that Ms. Rice's appointment has reinvigorated the influence and importance of the State Department...

From the start, America's first black woman Secretary of State promised to put diplomacy at the forefront of US foreign policy, and so far has largely remained true to her word.[113]

Forbes magazine has repeatedly named and placed Rice on its list of the most powerful women in the world.

With her steely nerves and delicate manners, Rice … has reinvigorated her position with diplomatic activism, whether it's promoting Israel's withdrawal from the Gaza Strip to ease the Palestinian conflict, or encouraging six-party talks

A Single Woman in the Nation's Capital

During her years in Washington, Rice has had numerous relationships but maintains her single status. Remaining single, Rice claims, allows her to devote nearly 100 percent of her energy and time to her all-consuming job.

Today, Rice has an apartment home in the Watergate complex along the banks of the Potomac River. She still has the Steinway piano her parents gave her years earlier, and she plays every day. She spends several hours a week working on her physical fitness, watches football on television, and enjoys jigsaw puzzles, an obsession she shares with George and Laura Bush. There is usually a large puzzle in the works at Camp David.

She spends a lot of her leisure time with the Bushes, whom she considers her extended family. She continues to make frequent trips to Camp David with the president, as well as visits to Bush's Texas ranch and to the senior Bush's home in Maine. She also spends time with her aunt Genoa McPhatter, who has a home in Norfolk, Virginia. If Rice can't get to Norfolk, McPhatter often makes the drive to Washington to deliver homemade Sunday dinners for her niece.

to get North Korea to stop its pursuit of nuclear weapons, or trying to stop Sudan's genocide.[114]

Despite her many successes and continuing popularity, Rice, along with the Bush administration, faces immense problems. One of Rice's strengths, however, has always been her positive outlook. Under Secretary of State Nicolas Burns, in charge of overseeing American foreign policy overseas, is one of many individuals who serve in the state department. Called under secretaries, these individuals are in charge of various departments and report directly to Rice. Burns spoke of Rice in February 2007: "Condi has a very positive frame of mind in the way she looks at the world... She's someone who believes every problem has a resolution."[115]

Introduction: From Birmingham to Washington

1. Quoted in Antonia Felix. *Condi: The Condoleezza Rice Story*. New York: New Market Press, 2002, p. 1.
2. Felix. *Condi: The Condoleezza Rice Story*, p. 218.
3. Quoted in Dick Morris and Eileen McGann. *Condi vs. Hillary: The Next Great Presidential Race*. New York: Regan Books, 2005, p. 64.
4. Morris and McGann. *Condi vs. Hillary*, p. 64.
5. Felix. *Condi: The Condoleezza Rice Story,* p. 17.

Chapter 1: A Child Prodigy

6. Morris and McGann. *Condi vs. Hillary,* page 74.
7. Felix. *Condi: The Condoleezza Rice Story,* p. 34.
8. Quoted in Felix. *Condi: The Condoleezza Rice Story,* p. 31.
9. Quoted in Felix. *Condi: The Condoleezza Rice Story,* p. 37.
10. Morris and McGann. *Condi vs. Hillary,* p. 66.
11. Quoted in Felix. *Condi: The Condoleezza Rice Story,* p. 60.
12. Quoted in Mike Knepler. "Aunt G.'s Favorite Niece: Condoleezza Rice." *The Virginian Pilot,* March 13, 2002.
13. Felix. *Condi: The Condoleezza Rice Story,* p. 37.
14. Quoted in Knepler. "Aunt G.'s Favorite Niece."
15. Quoted in Felix. *Condi: The Condoleezza Rice Story,* p. 42.
16. "Birmingham Native Condoleezza Rice Confirmation Vote Delayed." *Birmingham Times,* January 20, 2005.
17. Quoted in "Profile: Condoleezza Rice." *BBC News,* March 30, 2006. http://news.bbc.co.uk/2/hi/americas/3609327.stm.
18. Condoleezza Rice. "Remarks at Vanderbilt." *The White House,* May 13, 2004. www.whitehouse.gov/news/releases/2004/05/20040517.
19. Quoted in Arthur Herstein. "Acorns to Oaks." *World and I,* August 1, 2005.
20. Rice. "Remarks at Vanderbilt."
21. Rice. "Remarks at Vanderbilt."

22. Quoted in Felix. *Condi: The Condoleezza Rice Story*, p. 59.

23. Quoted in Felix. *Condi: The Condoleezza Rice Story*, p. 68.

24. James Mann. *Rise of the Vulcans: The History of Bush's War Cabinet*. New York: Viking, 2004, p. 147.

Chapter 2: Finding Her Passion

25. Quoted in Herstein. "Acorns to Oaks."

26. Quoted in Felix. *Condi: The Condoleezza Rice Story*, p. 74.

27. Condoleezza Rice. "Commencement Address at Boston College." *US Department of State*, May 22, 2006. www.state. gov/secretary/rm/2006/66630.htm.

28. Quoted from Knepler. "Aunt G.'s Favorite Niece."

29. Quoted in Felix. *Condi: The Condoleezza Rice Story*, p. 75.

30. Guy Raz. "For Albright and Rice, Josef Korbel is the Tie that Binds." *NPR*, June 28, 2006. www.npr.org/templates/story/ story.php?storyID=5516648

31. Quoted in Michael Dobbs. "Josef Korbel's Enduring Foreign Policy Legacy." *Washington Post*, December 28, 2000. www. rider.edu/~phanc/Phanc/JoKorbel.htm.

32. Felix. *Condi: The Condoleezza Rice Story*, p. 80.

33. Quoted in Morris. *Condi vs. Hillary*, p. 65.

34. Rice. "Remarks at Vanderbilt."

35. Quoted in Herstein. "Acorns to Oaks."

36. Quoted in Felix. *Condi: The Condoleezza Rice Story*, p. 93.

37. Felix. *Condi: The Condoleezza Rice Story*, p. 87.

38. Felix. *Condi: The Condoleezza Rice Story*, p. 97.

39. Felix. *Condi: The Condoleezza Rice Story*, p. 114.

40. Quoted in Felix. *Condi: The Condoleezza Rice Story*, p. 103.

Chapter 3: Professor Rice Goes to Washington

41. Herstein. "Acorns to Oaks."

42. Quoted in Felix. *Condi: The Condoleezza Rice Story*, p. 121.

43. Felix. *Condi: The Condoleezza Rice Story*, p. 118.

44. Mann. *Rise of the Vulcans*, p.146.

45. Quoted in Mann. *Rise of the Vulcans*, p. 146.

46. Quoted in Felix. *Condi: The Condoleezza Rice Story*, p. 6.

47. Quoted in George Bush and Brent Scowcroft. *A World Transformed.* New York: Alfred A. Knopf, 1998, p. 36.

48. Mann. *Rise of the Vulcans*, p. 171.

49. Quoted in Bush. *A World Transformed*, p. 41.

50. Quoted in Morris. *Condi vs. Hillary*, p. 103.

51. Quoted in Morris. *Condi vs. Hillary*, p. 106.

52. Morris. *Condi vs. Hillary*, p. 101.

53. Quoted in Morris. *Condi vs. Hillary*, p. 104.

54. Quoted in Felix. *Condi: The Condoleezza Rice Story*, p. 152.

55. Quoted in Felix. *Condi: The Condoleezza Rice Story*, p. 149.

Chapter 4: Provost Rice Advises the Candidate

56. Quoted in Felix. *Condi: The Condoleezza Rice Story*, p. 154.

57. Quoted in Morris. *Condi vs. Hillary*, p. 68.

58. Quoted in Felix. *Condi: The Condoleezza Rice Story*, p. 173.

59. Morris. *Condi vs. Hillary*, p. 112.

60. Quoted in Morris. *Condi vs. Hillary*, p. 113.

61. Quoted in Morris. *Condi vs. Hillary*, p. 113.

62. Tony Cox. "Professor Kiron Skinner discusses Condoleezza Rice." *NPR Special*, January 18, 2005.

63. Quoted in Herstein. "Acorn to Oaks."

64. Herstein. "Acorn to Oaks."

65. Quoted in Morris. *Condi vs. Hillary*, p. 116.

66. Quoted in Jim Puzzanghera. "Condoleezza Rice Returns to Stanford." *Knight Ridder/Tribune News Service*, June 15, 2002.

67. Quoted in Felix. *Condi: The Condoleezza Rice Story*, p. 161.

68. Quoted in Felix. *Condi: The Condoleezza Rice Story*, p. 188.

69. Quoted in Felix. *Condi: The Condoleezza Rice Story*, p. 189.

70. Quoted in Felix. *Condi: The Condoleezza Rice Story*, p. 190.

71. Morris. *Condi vs. Hillary*, p. 123.

72. Mann. *Rise of the Vulcans*, p. 250.

73. Bob Woodward. *State of Denial: Bush at War, Part III*. New York: Simon and Schuster, 2006, p. 9.

74. Quoted in Felix. *Condi: The Condoleezza Rice Story*, p. 12.

75. Condoleezza Rice. "Campaign 2000: Promoting the National Interest." *Foreign Affairs*, January/February 2000. www.foreignaffairs.org/20000101faessay5/condoleezza-rice/campaign-2000-promoting-the-national-interest.html.

76. Quoted in "Condoleezza Rice Delivers Remarks at Republican National Convention." *Washington Transcript Service*, August 1, 2000.
77. Quoted in Felix. *Condi: The Condoleezza Rice Story*, p. 2.

Chapter 5: National Security Advisor

78. Quoted in Felix. *Condi: the Condoleezza Rice Story*, p. 19.
79. Elizabeth Bumiller. "Bush's Right Hand Woman." *New York Times Upfront*, March 22, 2004.
80. Quoted in James Bamford. *A Pretext for War.* New York: Doubleday, 2004, p. 261.
81. Quoted in Morris. *Condi vs. Hillary*, p. 133.
82. Morris. *Condi vs. Hillary*, p. 124.
83. Quoted in Morris. *Condi vs. Hillary*, p. 69.
84. Quoted in Michael Elliott and Massimo Calabresi. "Is Condi the Problem?" *Time*, April 5, 2004.
85. Quoted in Felix. *Condi: The Condoleezza Rice Story*, p. 195.
86. Quoted in Felix. *Condi: The Condoleezza Rice Story*, p. 196.
87. Quoted in Neal Conan. "Condoleezza Rice's Testimony before the 9-11 Commission." *NPR: Talk of the Nation*, April 8, 2004.
88. Quoted in Neal Conan. "Condoleezza Rice's Testimony before the 9-11 Commission."
89. Quoted in Micah L. Sifry and Christopher Cerf. *The Iraq War Reader: History, Documents, Opinions.* New York: Simon and Schuster, 2003, p. 452.
90. Quoted in Sifry. *The Iraq War Reader,* p. 281.
91. Quoted in "Condoleezza Rice." *Source Watch.*
92. Quoted in Calvin M. Logue and Lynn M. Messina. *Representative American Speeches: 2002–2003.* New York: H.W. Wilson Company, 2003, p. 32.
93. Quoted in Scott Simon. "Condoleezza Rice's Appointment to Head the New Iraq Stabilization." *NPR: Talk of the Nation,* October 7, 2003.
94. Quoted in Simon. "Condoleezza Rice's Appointment to Head the New Iraq Stabliziation."
95. Quoted in Simon. "Condoleezza Rice's Appointment to Head the New Iraq Stabilization."

96. Felix. *Condi: The Condoleezza Rice Story,* p. 208.

97. Quoted in Morris. *Condi vs. Hillary,* pp. 127–28.

Chapter 6: Madam Secretary

98. Quoted in "Bush Picks Rice to Succeed Powell." *CNN.com* November 17, 2004. www.cnn.com/2004/ALLPOLITICS/11/16/rice.powell/index.html.

99. Quoted in Woodward. *State of Denial,* p. 377.

100. "Lieberman Statement." *Capitol Hill Press Releases,* January 25, 2005.

101. Quoted in Tony Cox. "Professor Kiron Skinner Discusses Condoleezza Rice." *NPR Special,* January 18, 2005.

102. Quoted in Cox. "Professor Kiron Skinner Discusses Condoleezza Rice."

103. Quoted in Palca. "Condoleezza Rice's Nomination to Take Over the State Department." [This is NEW – please give full details]

104. "Changing of the Guard at the State Department." *Miami Herald,* November 17, 2004.

105. Cox. "Professor Kiron Skinner Discusses Condoleezza Rice."

106. Quoted in "Remarks at the 88th Annual American Legion Convention." *US Department of State,* August 29, 2006. www.state.gov/secretary/rm/2006/71636.htm.

107. Quoted in Calvin M. Logue, Lynn M. Messina, and Jean DeHart. *Representative American Speeches: 2004-2005.* New York: H.W. Wilson, Company, 2005, p. 173–79.

108. Quoted in Woodward. *State of Denial,* p. 396.

109. Quoted in "Remarks at the 88th Annual American Legion Convention."

110. Quoted in Pam O'Toole. "Rice: Iran is Terrorism Banker." *BBC News,* February 17, 2006. http://news.bbc.co.uk/2/hi/americas/4722498.stm.

111. Quoted in "Introducing Condoleezza Rice." *Top Synergy,* October 8, 2006. www.topsynergy.com/famous-biography/Condoleezza_Rice.asp.

112. Quoted in "Secretary of State Condoleezza Rice." *US Department of State.* www.state.gov/secretary.

113. Jonathan Beale. "Rice Wins Praise After First Year." *BBC News*, December 28, 2005. http://news.bbc.co/uk/2/hi/americas/4565698.stm.

114. "Number One: Condoleezza Rice." *Forbes*, 2005. www.forbes.com/lists/2005/11/MTNG.html.

115. Quoted in Romesh Ratnesar and Elaine Shannon. "The Weight of the World." *Time*, February 12, 2007, p. 36.

November 14, 1954
Born in Birmingham, Alabama.

Fall 1970
After graduating two years early from high school, enrolls at the University of Denver.

1972
After a speech by Professor Josef Korbel on Russia, Rice changes her major to International Studies.

1972
Graduates from college and enrolls at the University of Notre Dame.

1976
Receives her Master's Degree and re-enrolls at the University of Denver for her doctorate.

1981
Receives her doctorate in International Studies and moves to California to join faculty at Stanford University.

1989
Joins President George H.W. Bush's administration as Director of Soviet and Eastern European Affairs.

March 1991
Returns to Stanford.

1993–1999
Serves as Provost at Stanford.

2000

Advises and then campaigns for George W. Bush during election.

January 22, 2001

Sworn in as National Security Advisor.

September 11, 2001

Terrorist attacks against the World Trade Center in New York City, and against The Pentagon in Washington D.C.

January 2005

Sworn in as Secretary of State.

Books

Hans Blix. *Disarming Iraq.* New York: Pantheon Books, 2004. Blix is the former United Nations Inspector for weapons of mass destruction in Iraq. He describes the search for weapons and the events leading to the invasion of Iraq.

Richard A. Clarke. *Against All Enemies: Inside America's War on Terror.* New York: Free Press, 2004. Former head of counterterrorism for twenty years reports on events leading up to 9/11 and the Bush administration's failure to heed the warnings.

Kevin Cunningham. *Condoleezza Rice: US Secretary of State.* Chanhassen, MN: The Child's World, 2005. An excellent biography of Rice.

Larry Diamond. *Squandered Victory: The American Occupation and the Bungled Effort to Bring Democracy to Iraq.* New York: Henry Holt and Company, 2005. The author, an expert on democracies, was asked by Rice to spend time in Iraq evaluating and advising the Iraqis in their transition to democracy.

Sandra J. Kachurek. *George W. Bush.* Berkeley Heights, NJ: Enslow Publishers, 2004. A good reference biography about President George W. Bush.

Marcus Mabry. *Twice as Good: Condoleezza Rice and Her Path to Power.* Emmaus, PA: Rodale Press, 2007. This biography of Rice tells of her birth, her education, her years at Stanford, as well as her years in government.

Mary Dodson Wade. *Condoleezza Rice: Being the Best.* Brookfield, CT: Millbrook Press, 2003 A good biography of Rice.

Periodicals

Michael Duffy. "Time 100: Condoleezza Rice: The Power of Proximity." *Time,* April 26, 2004. This magazine has a brief biography of Rice.

"Several Bridges to Build for Condoleezza Rice." *Detroit Free Press,* November 17, 2004. This article covers the need for Rice to rebuild America's diplomatic image.

Public Radio Resources

Melissa Block. "Career of Condoleezza Rice." *NPR: All Things Considered,* April 7, 2004. This radio program includes several interviews about Rice's life and career in politics.

Tony Cox. "Susan Rice discusses Condoleezza Rice." *NPR Special.* January 18, 2005. This radio interview with a political analyst includes the analyst's opinions about Rice.

Bob Edwards. "Condoleezza Rice Discusses the Administration's Stance on Iraq." *NPR: Morning Edition,* March 12, 2003. This radio interview with Rice covers the Bush administration's position on the Iraq war and the efforts to stabilize that country.

Ed Gordon. "Whether the Appointment of Condoleezza Rice as US Secretary of State Benefits Blacks Globally." *NPR: Special,* February 25, 2005. A series of interviews with black analysts and politicians about the effectiveness of Rice in promoting African Americans around the world.

Renee Montagne. "Secretary of State Condoleezza Rice Discusses How She Believes the World Views the United States." *NPR: Morning Edition,* May 27, 2005. This interview with Rice focuses on Rice's view of the need for diplomacy throughout the world.

Lynn Neary. "Confirmation Hearings for Condoleezza Rice." *NPR: Talk of the Nation,* January 18, 2005. This radio program includes a review of the confirmation hearings for Rice's appointment as Secretary of State.

Internet Resources

Jonathan Beale. "Warrior Princess to White House?" *BBC News,* January 25, 2006. http://news.bbc.co.uk/2/hi/americas/4628998.stm. This article recounts the move to urge Rice to run for president in 2008.

Emma Beck. "Growing up with Condoleezza Rice." *BBC News.* http://news.bbc.co.uk/2/hi/americas/4302605.stm. This article covers Rice's early life.

"Biography of Dr. Condoleezza Rice." *The White House.* www. whitehouse.gov/nsc/ricebio.html. This is a brief biography of Rice published by the White House.

"Bush Picks Rice to Succeed Powell." *CNN.Com* November 17, 2004. www.cnn.com/2004/ALLPOLITICS/11/16/rice.powell/ index.html. This site includes a comparison of Colin Powell and Rice.

"Center for a New Generation." *Boys and Girls Clubs of the Peninsula.* www.bgcp.org/cng_programs.php. This is a site that describes the activities and purpose of one Boys and Girls Club.

Condoleezza Rice. "Why We Know Iraq is Lying." *The White House,* January 23, 2003. www.whitehouse.gov/news/releases/ 2003/01/20030123-1.html. An article by Rice that describes her belief that Iraq is hiding weapons of mass destruction.

"Condoleezza Rice Discusses the Bush administration." *The Tavis Smiley Show, National Public Radio.* June 13, 2003. www.npr. org/programs/tavis/transcripts/2003/jun/030613.rice.html. Rice is interviewed about the Bush administration.

Sylive Lanteaume. "Rice to Head to Middle East with Iran in her Sights." *Yahoo News.* January 12, 2007. http://sg.news.yahoo. com/070112/1/45xgi.html. This article discusses Rice's agenda in terms of Iran.

"National Security Council." *The White House.* www.whitehouse. gov/nsc. A brief description of the National Security Council and its history.

Calvin Woodward. "Lawmakers Grill Rice over the Iraq War." *Yahoo News.* January 12, 2007 www.abcnews.go.com/Politics/ wireStory?id-2788280. This article covers Rice's testimony before Congress about the continuing problems in Iraq.

Index

Abbas, Mahmoud, 80
ABC News, 54
Afghanistan, 32, 66, 68, 78, 83
Air Force Academy, the, 41
Alabama, 8, 10–12
Albright, Madeleine, 26, *26*
al-Qaeda, 65, 66–68, *69*, 70, 78
American Academy of Arts and
    Sciences, 54
American Legion Convention, 78
Aspen Music Festival, 23
Aspen Strategy Group, 53
Austin, Texas, 55

Bach, 13
Baton Rouge, Louisiana, 15
BBC, 84
Beale, Jonathan, 84
Beethoven, 13
Benes, Eduard, 26
Berlin, 40, 41
Berlin Wall, 40, *42*, 43
bin Laden, Osama, 66, 72
Birmingham Southern
    Conservatory of Music, 13
Birmingham, Alabama, 8, 10,
    12, *16*
Blix, Hans, 70
Boston College, 25
Boxer, Senator Barbara, 74
Brahm, 14
Brest, Paul, 44
Brewer, Moses, 16
Brinkley, George, 28, 29
Bumiller, Elizabeth, 59
Burns, Nicholas, 86
Bush Doctrine, the, *60*
Bush, George H.W., 8, 9, 37, 41,
    41, 45, 54

Bush, George W., 8, 9, 11, 55,
    57, *57*, 58, 59, 72, 76
Bush, Laura, 85
Byrd, Senator Robert, 74

California, 33, 52
Camp David, 85
Carnegie Mellon University, 77
Carter, Jimmy, 32
Caspar, President Gerhard, 47,
    49, 54
CBS, 14, 70
Center for International Security
    and Arms Control, 33
Charlotte, North Carolina, 10
Cheney, Richard, 60, 64
Chevron Oil Company, 50
China, 61, *62*, 82
CIA, 59, 61, 66
Civil War, *11*
Clarke, Richard A., 66–68
Clinton, President Bill, *26*
Coalition Provisional Authority,
    71
Cold war, 28, 29, 32, 38, *40*,
    41, *42*, 43, 45, 53, 56
Communism, 24, 25–27, 28,
    31, 32, 84
Congress, 66, 75
Constitution Hall, 14
Council of Foreign Affairs, the,
    37
Cox, Tony, 51
Cyrillic, 27, 35
Czech, 25, 26, 27
Czechoslovakia, 31

Democrat, 32
Denver Bronco, 21, 44

Denver, Colorado, 20, 26, 29
Denver Symphony Orchestra, 21
Department of International Relations, 26
Department of State, 31
Director of Soviet and Eastern European Affairs, 38

East Germany, 43
Eastern Europe, 29, 39, 40, 47
Elizabeth II, Queen, 41
ESPN, 21
Europe, 39, 47
Eutaw, Alabama, 11

Faculty Incentive Fund, 52
Fairfield Industrial High School, 10
Fairfield, 10
FBI, 66
Federal Advisory Committee, 53
Felix, Antonia, 8, 9, 12, 15, 27, 29, 32, 34, 44, 50, 72
Forbes (magazine), 85
Ford, President Gerald, 37, 41
Ford, Susan, 53
France, 78, 82

Gates, Robert, 61
Gaza Strip, 80, 85
Gelb, Leslie, 76
Gerasamenko, Dmitri, 30
Germany, 26, 42, 43, 45, 54, 82
Germany Unified and Europe Transformed (book), 54
Glasnost, 39
Gorbachev Era, The (book), 54
Gorbachev, Mikhail, 38, 39, 41, 43, 45
Great Britain, 82

Hastorf, Provost Albert, 35
Head, Julia, 11

Head Start, 12
Herstein, Arthur, 33, 51
Hewlett-Packard, 50
Holocaust, the, 26
Hoover, Herbert, 36, 36
Hoover Institution on War, Revolution, and Peace, the, 36
Hoover Institution, the, 33, 36, 54, 55
Houston, Texas, 46
Hussein, Saddam, 69, 70, 71

Indiana, 28
Iran, 69, 81, 81, 82, 83
Iraq, 41, 69, 69, 70, 71, 72, 74, 78, 79, 81, 82, 83

Japan, 82
Jefferson, Thomas, 75
Johnson C. Smith University, 10
Joint Chiefs of Staff, 35, 59
J.P. Morgan, 50
Juilliard School of Music, 23

Kazakhstan, 50
Kennebunkport, Maine, 46, 55, 56, 85
Kerry, John, 72
Korbel, Josef, 24, 24, 25, 26
Kremlin, 30, 31
Ku Klux Klan, 18, 19

Lamont School of Music, 23
Lemman, Nicholas, 71
Lieberman, Senator Joe, 74
London, 26
Los Angeles, 71
Los Angeles Times (newspaper), 50

Malta, 41, 43
Mann, James, 22, 35, 38, 56
Mateska, Mark, 65

McGann, Eileen, 9, 12, 13, 14, 43, 49, 55, 61
Mcnair, Denise, 18
McPhatter, Genoa (aunt), 15, 25, 85
Miami Herald (newspaper), 76
Middle East, 71, 78, 79, *80*, 81, 82, 97
Morgan, Senator Becky, 54
Morgenthau, Hans, 31
Morris, Dick, 9, 12, 13, 14, 43, 49, 55, 61
Mustafa Fuzer Nawi, 14

National Football League, 21
National Medal of Arts and National Humanities Medals, 14
National Review (newspaper) 58
National Security Advisor, 9, 37, 41, *41*, 56, *59*, 61, 62, 68, 72, 73, 75
National Security Council, 38, 64, 65, 66, 71
Nazi, 26
Nazism, 25, 27
New York City, 23
New York Times (newspaper), 70
9/11 Commission, 66, 68
Nixon, Richard M., 41
Nordlinger, Jay, 57
Norfolk, Virginia, 85
North Korea, 69, 82–83, *82*, 86

Palestine, *80*
Palo Alto, California, 33
Paris, 26, 78
Pennsylvania, 64, 77
Pentagon, the, 31, 35, 64
Perestroika, 39
Phi Beta Kappa, 27
Pittsburgh, Pennsylvania, 77
Poland, 40

Politics Among Nations (book), 31
Potomac River, 85
Powell, Colin, 64, 72, *73*
Pravda, 32
Presbyterian, 10–12
Presidential Medal of Freedom, 41
Principals Committee, 59, 64
Push, Stephen, 68
Puzzanghera, Jim, 67

Raisian, John, 55
Rand Corporation, the, 31, *36*, 50
Ray, Angelena (mother), 10, 12, 15, 16, 17
Ray, Mattie (grandmother), 12, *13*
Raz, Guy, 25
Realpolitik, 31
Republican, 32, 41
Republican National Convention, 54, 56, *57*
Republican Party (political party), 32
Rice, Condoleezza, 8, 10, *26*, 38, 55, 58, 67, *73*, 76
  as a musician, 12–13, *14*, 15, 16, 20–22, 23
  on al-Qaeda, 68, 70, 78
  birth of, 10
  on democracy in the Middle East, 79
  as Director of Soviet and Eastern European Affairs, 38, 39, 40, 41–43, 45
  on family, 10, 11
  on fighting terrorism, 72, 76, 77, 81–82
  on fitness, *65*
  on football, 21
  on George W. Bush, 57
  on graduation day, 27–28
  on her faith, *67*

on international politics, 47
on Iraq and Saddam Hussein,
70, 71, 78, 81
on Korbel, 24, 25, 26, 27
as national security advisor,
59, 60, 61, 62, 63, 64, 65,
66, 67, 68–69, 70, 71, 72,
73, 75
on President Carter's foreign
policy, 32
as professor at the Stanford
University, 33, 34, 37, 48
as provost, 47, 48, 49–50, 51,
52, 54, 55
on reunification of Germany,
42, 43
on Russia, 24, 25, 30
as Secretary of State, 73,
74–76, 77, 78, 79–81, 82,
83, 85–86
on segregation, 17, 20
on the Palestinian-Israeli
conflict, 80
on the State Department,
83–84
Rice, John Wesley (father), 10,
11
Rumsfeld, Donald, 64, 72
Russia, 24, 25, 28, 29, 30, 31,
39, 43, 45, 82

San Francisco Bay earthquake,
49, 50
San Francisco 49er, 44
School of Humanities and
Sciences Dean's Award for
Distinguished Teaching, 34
Scowcroft, General Brent, 37,
38, 39, 41, 45, 56
Secretary of State, 9, 21, 26, 64,
72, 73, 73, 74, 75, 76, 78, 80,
82, 83, 85, 86
Secretary-General, 38

Senate, 74, 76, 82
Shannon, Elaine, 76
Six-Party talks, 82, 85
Sixteenth Baptist Church, 18
60 Minutes (TV Program), 14
Skinner, Kiron, 77
Slevin, Peter, 72
Solidarity Party (political party),
40
South Korea, 82
Southern University, 15
Soviet Communist Party (politi-
cal party), 38
Soviet Union, 8, 24, 25, 27, 28,
29, 30, 31, 32, 37, 38, 39, 40,
40, 43, 45, 50, 54, 61
St. Mary's Academy, 20, 20, 23
St. Petersburg, 30
Stalin, Josef, 24
Stanford University, 9, 33, 36,
44, 48
Steinway grand piano, 20, 85
Stillman College, 10, 11
Super Bowl, 21

Taliban, the, 66, 78
Tchaikovsky, Peter Ilyich, 30
Tennessee, 28
Texas, 46, 55, 60, 85
Texas Rangers, 55
Thomas, Evan, 60
Titusville, 19
Tolstoy, Leo, 55
Tuscaloosa, Alabama, 11

Uncertain Allegiance: The Soviet
Union and the Czechoslovak
Army (book), 54
United Nations, the, 70, 82
University of Denver, 20, 22,
23, 26, 27, 28, 29
University of Notre Dame, 28,
50
Upchurch, Rick, 21, 44

Vanderbilt University, 19, 28
Violin Sonata in D Minor
  (musical composition), 14
Virginia, 74, 85

Walter J. Gores Award for
  Excellence in Teaching, 34
Washington, D.C., 8, 14, 31,
  35, 38
Washington, Gene, 44
Washington Post (newspaper), 72
West Bank, 80
West Point, 41
Westminster Presbyterian
  Church, 12

White House, the, 8, 59, 64, 65
Wilson, Governor Pete, 52
Woodward, Bob, 56
Woolworth's, 17
World Trade Center, 63
World War II, the, 26, 27, 28,
  31, 84

Yeltsin, Boris, 43, 45
Yo-Yo Ma, *14*
Yugoslavia, 26

Zelikow, Philip, 54

Anne Wallace Sharp is the author of the adult book *Gifts,* a compilation of stories about hospice patients, several children's books, including *Daring Pirate Women,* and eleven other Thomson Gale books. In addition, she has written numerous magazine articles for both the adult and juvenile market. A retired registered nurse, Sharp has a degree in history. Her other interests include reading, traveling, and spending time with her two grandchildren, Jacob and Nicole. Sharp lives in Beavercreek, Ohio.